PASSION
SUCCESS PROSPERITY

ENTREPRENEUR

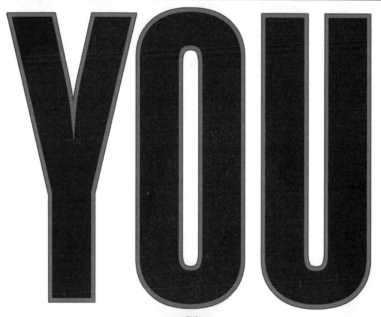

YOU

HOLLY KATKO

Publisher's Cataloging in Publication

Entrepreneur you : how to make the jump to business
    ownership and live your life with passion, success and
    prosperity! / Holly Katko.
      p. cm.
      Includes index.
      LCCN 2011931462
      ISBN-13: 9781937158002
      ISBN-10: 1937158004

      1. Entrepreneurship.   2. Success in business.
    I. Title.

HB615.K38 2011   658.4'21
                    QBI11-600111

ATTENTION: QUANTITY DISCOUNTS ARE AVAILABLE TO YOUR COMPANY, EDUCATIONAL INSTITUTION OR ASSOCIATION

For reselling, educational purposes, subscription incentives, gifts or fundraising campaigns.

For more information, please contact the publisher at

U-Connect, Inc.
630/963-3630
www.uconnectsite.com

Editor: *Elizabeth Carter* of Freelance Writing Solutions | www.FreelanceWritingSolutions.com

Cover Design by *George Foster* | www.fostercovers.com

Inside Book Design and Layout by *Sandy Stenson* of Stenson Graphix | www.StensonGraphix.com

TABLE OF CONTENTS

This book is dedicated to my mother and father, for raising me to think on my own and for instilling a strong work ethic. To my daughter who would stay up late at night and listen to my stories and help me build programs even when she was only nine years old. And to my husband who has always encouraged me to go to the next level and never ever give up.

God gives you an arm full of talents. When He takes one away from you, don't cling to it — for He will give you another in place of it.

Written by Emily Smith at the age of 9.

PROLOGUE

Entrepreneurship. I just like to say the word. It means so much! It means you're in control of your own destiny. You make the dreams and set the goals. You're in charge! The decision to own your own business is one of the most worthwhile decisions you'll ever make. I believe in entrepreneurism with my heart, body and soul. I *know* this is the journey for you. You're on your way, and no one can stop you!

Who should read this book? Anyone who believes life holds something more for them, anyone who is ready to take control of their lives, YOU who are ready to move out from under an employer's foot and onto the wings of entrepreneurship.

Why read this book? Because you've already decided that it's time for a change — in a big way. Entrepreneurism can be a change, all right — especially if you've never ventured into business ownership before! In this book, I share with you the guidance, support and encouragement you need. And with the tools and exercises that lie on these pages, trust me — you can do *anything*. Entrepreneurism empowers you to take the first step to the rest of your life. Make your dreams of independence reality. There isn't a thing in this world like the feeling of owning your own business...the excitement of knowing that you're making all the decisions...that there is no one to answer to...that you own the results, good or bad.

The world is open before you, so don't hold back. Go for it! This is exciting stuff, and I want you to get excited about it!

As you read this book, you'll gain a clear sense of your purpose in life, something that so many people never experience (such a shame and such a waste). You'll learn how to embrace entrepreneurism and how to take this path for everything it's worth. You'll complete exercises that give you the tools you'll need to succeed. And through it all, you'll find that this is an unforgettable and oh-so rewarding journey. As you move forward to the next level in your life, you'll enjoy deep feelings — excitement, confidence, exhilaration! — that may have been missing in your life until now.

You may find that the path to entrepreneurism isn't necessarily quick and it's not always easy. Your steps may be tenuous at first. You may be scared. It's okay. I'm going to guide you along your way. You can do this!

It's time to make a difference in your life and in the lives of those around you. Don't let life pass you by. Become the entrepreneur you're meant to be.

Enjoy the Freedom of Entrepreneurship. The time is now.

INTRODUCTION

I always knew I would own my own business, but for a long, long while, I was afraid to go out on my own. Not until the year 2000, after many years in a corporate environment, did I have the revelation. It was then that I really understood what I wanted to do.

Out of the blue, I felt a jolt, like lightening going through me. It was one of the most important moments of my life. All of a sudden my destiny was revealed; there it was in front of me. ENTREPRENEURSHIP IS ME! In one fell swoop, I could see what I was supposed to do. I was going to be an entrepreneur, and even more than that, I was going to help other people fulfill their own dreams of becoming entrepreneurs, too.

I realized this was not someone else's plan. These were not someone else's thoughts. These thoughts were mine, and mine alone! I tried to explain this excitement within me to my loved ones, but I found that no one could truly feel the same excitement I felt. I also realized that no one could help me to fulfill my destiny. Yes, I could talk about my dream with other people and have them share their feedback with me, but no one could make my destiny happen for me — but me.

"Yes," I thought, "I'm finally on my way, and what a great opportunity and ability I have TO MAKE IT HAPPEN. The universe is mine and I am the universe. I'm finally able to give my full power to what I know."

I had worked in corporate America for large and small companies for more than 20 years. I had helped build small companies and helped open divisions of large companies to make them even larger. The excitement of selling and building cutting-edge products and services helped me become the entrepreneur I am today.

And yet even before that, I was destined for entrepreneurship. I was raised on a farm in Iowa where we worked from dawn until dusk. The work was hard, no doubt about it. But from the time I was old enough to talk, I realized that owning my own business was the only way to make my own money, have full ownership of my life, and create opportunities based upon my ideals and perspectives.

I was always the pioneer. If someone told me to do something one way, I would do it the opposite. (I'm sure there may be a psychological defect there, but heck, it worked for me!) I would constantly search for new and different ways to make a product or service work. I always tried to build what the customer wanted, not what we wanted the customer to have. Of course, in the corporate world, fitting the norm was more important than trying to build a better mouse trap!

So this begs the question, do you want to be the mouse holding the cheese or the mouse nervously checking out the trap someone else has built, not knowing when it will snap closed? It's your choice. Do you want to feel "the jolt" of your lifetime? Do you want to be able to open your door and say — this is all mine? Do you want to know you have created your own destiny and feel the pride in knowing you made it happen? Then let's go! You're about to embark on the journey of your life time!

HOW TO USE THIS BOOK

It is my sincere hope that this book not only inspires you, but also shows you how to put your dreams into action.

With that in mind, throughout the pages of this book I've included hands-on, thought-provoking exercises that will hopefully prompt you to realize how **everything you're reading fits directly into your life**. Some of the exercises will take you only a few seconds, while others may require more careful contemplation. All of the exercises are numbered sequentially, according to chapter. They are indexed at the back of this book for easy reference.

I have also included an easy-to-recognize icon in the margins of the pages, to help you get the most out of this book. As you read, look for:

 The words "Do It Now!" indicate areas where you need to take action now to get moving; don't wait until you're done reading the book!

And finally, please visit my website **www.uconnectsite.com** to follow me on Facebook, Twitter and LinkedIn and to sign up for my blog. Join the conversation, and become part of a vibrant community of fellow entrepreneurs who are all living their dreams!

CHAPTER 1

READY...SET...GO!
DEFINING YOUR COMPANY
Embrace Your Opportunities

I WAS RECENTLY AT A SEMINAR AND HEARD A REMARKABLE WOMAN SPEAK: Maureen Beal, owner of National Van Lines. She said she never aspired as a little girl to own a multi-million dollar company. She dreamt of being a ballerina. But life threw her a different opportunity, and she grabbed it.

National Van Lines is family-owned business headquartered in suburban Chicago. Maureen had been living in Los Angeles, and moving to Illinois really wasn't part of her plan. But circumstances had changed within the company, and it was clear that someone new needed to take the reins. Even though she had two older brothers, Maureen was identified as the strong one — the one who understood why they were in this business and who grasped the importance of serving the customer from the heart. She also realized that while one of her biggest strengths was her ability to implement a plan, she also needed to hire people who had the vision to provide the fresh new ideas that she couldn't come up with. Together, they were able to create and implement a strategy that has helped National Van Lines thrive. Maureen went on to say that owning the family business and running it has been the most rewarding experience of her life.

As she shared this story with us at the seminar, I realized that Maureen had found herself faced with a major change, and that she had embraced it fully...leading to a positive, life-affirming realization.

If it looks like an opportunity, take it! It is an opportunity — an opportunity to be in tune with your dreams. Take action. These moments of change are where the rubber meets the road.

You have the opportunity to enjoy the freedom of owning your own business. Wow, you don't realize what you're missing until you actually take that leap of faith in yourself! Yes, that's right, *faith in yourself.* No one can push you or prod you or make you do it. You need to do it for *you*!

You have the chance to become a great leader in your town, your nation, the world! Or...you can stay in that same job with the same hope that everything will be okay, and wait for your next performance review hoping they like the job you've done because you can't decide on your own if you've done a good job. I don't think so. Do you?! Or...you can sit at home if you don't have a job and wait for something to come to you and hope that opportunity will just come to your door if you simply pray long enough. Again, I don't think so. Don't wait for life to come to you. Get out there and do it.

It can be easy to stay in the same job, doing the same thing, because it makes us feel safe or because we have a family depending on us. But that safety is just an illusion.

After all, ask yourself, why you were put on this green earth? You're here to make things happen! And the best way to do this? Own your own business and be a thriving successful entrepreneur. So just do it. You'll hear me say this over and over again because that is the real secret to getting where you want to be and fulfilling your destiny in life. You must do it. You must take the first step, and the next step, and the next. No one can do this for you. The terrific thing is that you don't even need all your ducks in a row to become a successful entrepreneur! I'll show you in the next few pages as I tell my own story about how I started my company, you'll see that all you really need is the drive and passion to take action.

It's a great feeling waking up every day knowing you're the one who has built your business. It's exciting to know that you're helping others. It's wonderful to employ people and to help them earn enough money to take care of themselves and their families. I believe one of the greatest things about being an entrepreneur is the thrill of knowing you can help others by what you do. As long as you know you're helping others, you'll succeed.

WHAT PATTERNS IN YOUR LIFE HAVE BROUGHT YOU HERE?

At this point you may be feeling concerned because you know you want to own your own business, but you don't know what that business should be. Look at the patterns in your life. Notice how they all seem to join together to bring you to this place, equipped with the skills and tools you need here and now in your life.

These are the skills you'll use to build and strengthen your company. You are the dreamer to make your company a reality.

When I look at my own patterns, I notice that when I've worked for other people, I've always chosen to work for companies that are on the leading edge of their industries. I've always enjoyed the excitement of a new product, a new territory, a new company. I've always been drawn to something or someone who needed an entrepreneurial spirit to go out there and build that territory, product or staff. I thrive on living up to that next new challenge, that next new risk — except that I had always been sharing the value and the income from my successes. I'm done with that. Now that I'm an entrepreneur, I intend to keep all that income I generate, not just a percentage of the value.

When you look back on your life, it may seem like a zigzag pattern on nothingness. You may have done plenty of things in your life, but none of it may seem to fit together to form any sort of a pattern. You may ask yourself what you're doing here. What has your life been about? Why have you done the things you've done? Is there a reason behind all of this, and if so, how can you unveil the mystery behind the purpose of your life so far? Well, believe it or not, there is no great mystery to it! Even if you can't see it at the moment, trust me. Everything you've done in your life has prepared you for right now.

THE LAW OF ATTRACTION

Opportunity comes in many packages. The most important thing for you to do is to "put it out there." Make sure people know that you're looking for opportunity. Take action to bring opportunity into your life.

Then start looking for the opportunities you have asked for. **Simply open your** (DINI) **eyes.** We get used to looking at things through our own self-monitoring ways. What didn't look like an opportunity before can look like one now — if you're looking for it.

Having a bad boss, or crashing your car, or having to take another college class ten years after graduating from college (just a few of my own life lessons) — all are lessons that we learn from. But not only are we learning from these lessons, some day and in some way they will apply to what you're doing now. So recognize the opportunities. Many opportunities crossing your path now are based on something you have learned many years ago.

Have you ever had something unexpected happen to you and, because of a prior experience, you knew how to handle it? Recognizing opportunity ties easily into change. Change is a part of everyone's lives, so now it's time to turn change into an opportunity. Whereas we may think change is a scary thing, it's simply a different version of something we already know. Or maybe, if we're lucky enough, it's a brand new experience — something we have never done before, expanding our horizons and broadening our opportunities.

 Don't dismiss any opportunity. **Look at every opportunity you see,** and keep your eyes open for more. You might start your company by going in several different directions — and I say try them all out, then narrow your scope. Every person, every job, every product or service has been put in your path for a reason. Don't dismiss anything without reviewing it closely. There may be a jewel in there, and you may miss it because your focus is too narrow or because it's a new concept you don't understand yet. Realize that you, like everyone else, came from an environment that was more closed; you now have an opportunity to open these paths and explore other options. You'll learn that you're far from alone in this endeavor. Go to my website (**www.uconnectsite.com**) and get connected with other business owners through our blog. Share your stories as we all continue to grow our businesses. You'll notice that many people have founded their own companies using skills they never imagined they would use for this purpose.

You may find that it's time to shift gears completely and do something you've never done before. That doesn't mean you throw out your past; it simply means you have to transfer your skills over to a new situation and the new company you're building. For example, when I was young I always wanted to become an actress, to be on the stage and perform. Well, believe it or not, that dream has come true in a way, but not how I thought it would. You see, I was always deathly afraid of public speaking. Because of this fear, I took up public speaking. Now I speak for a living. I'm on the stage helping others obtain their dreams. You can do it too!

EXERCISE 1.1

Make a list of all the dreams you've had in your life. I want you to think big. Just don't blow past this exercise. This is the beginning of starting your company. Write down every dream, from when you were a child to now. Did you want to become an astronaut, the President of the United States, a fireman, a nurse? Write down every single dream. Circle those that you still want, that you wish you had in your life right now. How can you make those dreams a reality? Are you making them a reality now and you just don't recognize them for what they are?

EXERCISE 1.1 *continued*

Keep this list close at hand throughout reading this book and refer to it often. This list of dreams will be the basis for starting your company. The more you look at it, the more the opportunities will come. Talk about your dreams to others. No matter how impossible your dreams may sound write them down now. You will be amazed how they will come alive. If you want it bad enough, you'll get it. Maybe not in exactly the way you picture it right now, but if you keep working for it, you'll get what you ask for.

As you start getting the hang of recognizing opportunities, you'll probably find more than one. Try them all. See how they fit you. Don't throw them out without taking a good hard look at what they are offering you. What I have found is that by trying out many opportunities over time, I have become very good at recognizing which opportunities are right for me and which are not. With practice, I've learned to focus on those opportunities that will bring me the money I expect and the resources I need to get there.

Identify Your Options

A friend of mine owns a nice, growing company. She started out as a secretary, and a very good one at that. A lot of the work was very detail-oriented: writing letters, making travel arrangements, formulating agendas, and creating proposals and worksheets. No one within the company she worked for really liked to do that kind of work. She came to realize that with her expertise, she could easily provide this service to other companies in addition to the one where she was working at the time. And so she started her company, by providing these services to a single small business where the owner just didn't have time to keep his administrative house in order. After a while she found another business in need of her services, and another. Pretty soon she realized that she didn't have time to do all the work and build her business, so she hired dependable people with good skills. She got terrific results by hiring people who wanted to work part-time from home and who understood the value of a job well done. She briefly considered outsourcing these services from another country to increase her margins, but she decided she wasn't comfortable that this would provide the same high quality of service to her clients. Now, at the time that I'm writing this, my friend has dedicated employees throughout the nation providing administrative services for her clients on an as-needed basis, freeing the client from incurring the cost and liability of full-time employees performing these services. This is a $5 million company. Not bad!

You'll note that this friend started her company while employed by another. She found this gave her the security she needed until she knew her company would be strong enough to support her needs. Which it does...and more!

WHERE IS THE NEED?

One of the ways to start your business is to find a job or task that no one else likes to do. Simply put, if a task isn't someone's core area of expertise, or if it can be inconvenient, difficult, or cost-prohibitive to do themselves, then people may consider hiring someone else to do it for them.

(DINI) **Dig deep into your skills and abilities** and look for potential products or services in which you have an expertise that fills a need. Find a product or service that fixes a problem or makes someone else's job easier. Where there is pain, there is gain in the business world. If you can identify an area where people need help and you can provide the solution, you'll enjoy great success.

WHAT ARE YOUR STRENGTHS?

At the time that I had the "jolt" I talked about in the introduction, I had just turned 40, had paid my mortgage off and had saved $10,000 in the bank to start my business. I said to myself, "If I don't do it now, it will be another five years, and then another five years, and then another...STOP!"

Once I got off of my own hamster wheel and stopped spinning myself around in a flurry of "cant's" and "not good enoughs", I realized no one was torturing me or making me stay put in my current job but me. I just needed to take that first step — to realize I was good enough, to realize I was my hardest judge and that I had skills that no one else could match. I was special. I was made different from anyone else on this planet, and no one could match my talents and my abilities to obtain clients and grow a successful, thriving business like I could.

I decided to make a list of all the things I had done since the beginning of my 20+ year career in the business world. I was surprised at how many skills I came up with. I had been raised on a working farm, worked as an industrial safety director, managed sales teams, created products and services, traveled across the country, learned computer skills and much more. You'll be surprised, as you take your own inventory of skills, how much you have to offer the world.

Look at all the options around you. Let's say you want to start your own business
but you have absolutely no idea what you want to do. Think about all the things
you can do. You've been on this planet long enough to have done some construc-
tive things. I did everything from hard labor on the farm to presenting and selling
products to Fortune 50 companies.

Maybe your skills could be as simple as knowing how to shine a pair of shoes until
they sparkle. In fact, I know of an entrepreneur who did just that.

He started with nothing. His family left him because he couldn't hold down a job,
and he sank into depression. He asked his father for an answer to this dilemma.
His father told him, "Well, you can shine shoes, can't you?" So he did just that. He
started shining shoes at O'Hare Airport in Chicago. After a while, the old shoeshine man at the station next to him retired, and he took over that stand, and
soon another stand, and another. He looked at all the people who needed their
shoes shined, and he expanded his business even further. He shined shoes for
customers waiting for their cars to be checked in at car dealers. He shined shoes
for prospective buyers at trade shows, and now he's looking at working with large
companies where image is important and a pair of shined shoes is critical to top
off the uniform. Shining shoes was more than just a job for him; he looked at it as
an opportunity to build a successful and growing business. He now owns a half-
million dollar company. What did it take? A skill, done well.

You can do this too, by focusing on prior, current and to-be-created skills. Do you
think this man had a passion for shining shoes? No, but he did have a passion to
become a successful entrepreneur. He has never given up. Fulfilling the dream
of owning a business is what it's all about. This man had a skill, and he found
a need — a job most people couldn't be bothered to do — that turned out to be
a great fit for him.

WHAT ARE YOUR PASSIONS?

When I realized I wanted to become an entrepreneur, all I knew was that I wanted
to own my own company and be successful at it. Beyond that, I didn't really know
what my passions were. But I knew I wanted to find a service or a product that would
fill a need, relieve people of their pain — and generate income immediately and
continually throughout the years.

That was when I realized that my passion was to fulfill the mission of "Service
above Self", and so that's where I started. I began developing seminars, books and
other training services to help people reach the next level in their lives. And as I did

this, I could feel myself come alive. As long as you're building a product or service that will help others and eliminate a pain, you can't lose. Your product will soar once you find the right market.

Not all people know what their passion is when they start their own business. Or they may know what their passion is, but they're not sure how they can make an income from it. For example, I'm passionate about the study of insects. Could I make a living as an entrepreneur based on this passion? Sure I could. But I would have to get the best cameras, equipment, and labs. I would have to travel the world to find the most unique insects not yet discovered. I would need more education, money, sponsors...could I do this? Of course I could. But more importantly, do I want it bad enough? I also love gardening. If I wanted to pursue this passion, I could start a landscape business. I would need land, a building, and money to purchase inventory and hire staff. No, I probably wouldn't do that either (even though it is one of my passions). Passions and starting your own company can be synonymous... or not.

You're the one to decide. Are you so passionate about something that you could focus all of your energy on that one thing? Even if you have a husband, wife, children, a mortgage, a car, or need money for the kids' college, retirement... on and on and on! Would you be willing to take that leap of faith to see if it works? We all have some level of prior commitments, whether to loved ones or financial goals that we feel obligated to fulfill. What are we willing to do to get where we need to go? Remember you're in this for the long haul — you won't be just a flash in the pan. You may not have a clear vision yet, but you do know entrepreneurship is the path you choose.

Keep your passion alive. You'll always do your best work if you're living in the zone. Living in the zone means feeling the passion within your work. When you own your own company, you'll find that work is no longer work; instead, you're turning your own dreams into reality.

WHAT WILL BRING IN INCOME?

Let's face it, the foundation for every strong company is money. There is no way of getting around this fact. If you don't have money, you can't have people working for you, you can't build your product, and you can't have the systems you need. Without money, it's pretty hard to get or stay in business.

Starting your company while employed by another

If you're currently employed and looking to start your new company, you may find it helpful or reassuring to establish a client base before you leave your other job. I know this is a difficult endeavor, and you may feel guilty doing this while working for another company, but it's important to always be looking ahead to the next level of your life. **If you want to start your new company, then do it now**. Of course, you won't be able to put 100% effort into your new company, but it can give you a great start, so that when you're ready to leave your old job, you already have a client base established. The most important thing to remember is to get that first client on the books and begin establishing long-term relationships. Shoot high and get the big guys on board now! From there, the rest is history. Follow the path you've laid for your success.

Finding the passion within the product

You would be amazed at the different types of businesses out there. If you're lucky enough to have a clear passion, do it. If you don't have a clear passion — still do it. Something. Anything. Get started anywhere you can. Don't sit and wait. The right opportunity will present itself when it's time.

If you're just not sure what to do, **find a product or service that will bring in income**. You may find that a product or service isn't your passion, but will pay the bills and will jump start you in the right direction. Do it! You may find a passion within the product or service — like the shoeshine man, even if you eventually find yourself on a different path than what you had originally chosen. You'll be surprised at life's opportunities if you just let them flow.

For example, one of my businesses is selling health insurance (**www.uconnectinsurance.com**). Do you think I had a passion to sell health insurance? Not at all. But it did bring in income, and I did ultimately find the passion within the product. Selling insurance actually helped me fulfill my mission of Service above Self. There was a need in the market, and I could use my expertise to help provide the solution.

I've seen a lot in my career, and I've learned so much more than I ever thought I would. I can say I've never been truly elated about what I did for a living until I started my own company. Never, when I was working for others, did I say to myself, "Wow, this is what I want to do for the rest of my life." Nonetheless, when I worked for other people, I would treat their business with the same care and respect as if it were my own; I would put my whole heart and soul into my work. I knew that if I didn't treat every job as if I owned the company, I would fail.

If you're drawn to a particular product or service but it's not necessarily your passion, then look deeper as to what's going on under the surface. Your passion may be an adjunct to the end product you're going to offer, but you might not be able to see this yet. If you're lucky enough to find that your passion can be a deliverable to a client, then do it. If your product offering isn't your passion, still do it.

 EXERCISE 1.2

Let's get to the bottom of this. Take the time NOW to really look at what you have done in your past that you can build on in the future.

Pull out your last resume, if you have one, and see what you've got on it. Or if you don't have one, create one now. Pretend you're about to hire yourself into the line of work you want your company to be in.

In your evaluation, start with the last five years:

What position(s) have you held?

What skills have you learned? Come up with at least 25 things. Have you obtained any certifications or licenses? For example, I maintained my life and health and property/casualty insurance license from 20 years ago — and I started my company based on that license. You may have a certificate or knowledge base in a particular area that others are willing to pay for. Even if you don't have a certificate or degree — the knowledge that you have gained through experience can mean as much if not more than that piece of paper.

Now review your list and circle those areas you feel you have the strongest expertise. Which ones would really bring about the change, the opportunity you have been waiting for? Look at all the things you have done in your life, and realize that each one of those skills was acquired so you could be where you are today.

Now go back through this list again and circle the things you like to do. There might be only one thing — there might be none. Don't worry. You aren't trying to impress anyone here; you are digging deep into what you can do.

What expertise can you share with someone else? For example, I was so amazed when I was able to draw upon my human resource background from 20 years ago and help employers develop employee handbooks or resolve high-level HR issues. I have found that many people just need an outside opinion to get them moving in the right direction, and they are willing to pay for it.

EXERCISE 1.2 *continued*

Now go back ten years (if this applies to you!), and perform the same exercise. Pick 25 skills that you obtained. What did you learn? What were you doing? Where were you in life's agenda? Were you starting a family, finishing a family, retiring, going to school? Not only are work skills important to write down, but also life skills — what did you learn and how can you share this with others and make money doing it?

For instance, people pay me to sit down and talk with them about where they are in life and how they can get to the next level in their careers or their companies, so they can move in the right direction. Why? Because I know how to get them to the next level in their lives, based upon my own life experiences. Guess what? You have many skills others are willing to pay for. Write them down now, quickly; take five minutes and do this.

I know for many of us going back ten years may sound like a long time, but to others it's just the tip of our experience. Keep repeating this set of exercises, going further and further back in time. Again, circle those areas where you feel you have honed a skill that you can bring into your business.

Now pick out your passions from this list. You might not recognize them. For me, my number one passion was to start my own business. It didn't matter what I sold — what mattered to me was that I had my own business.

Next, pick out which skills or areas of expertise can make you money right away, even if they're not your passions.

And now, let's pull it all together. Based on what you've learned about yourself, what would you like to do? What business, what product? Is there something you've always wanted to try? Take that interest and analyze the skills needed for that area. What skills could you bring into this new product or service? If you can't come up with a passion that would serve as the foundation for a good business, then turn to the skills that can bring in money. The point here isn't to wait; the point is to take action now!

TAKE ACTION NOW!

Your company will take many twists and turns as it grows, but you need to get started somewhere. Creativity is one of the prerogatives of the entrepreneur; you have the ability to build and rebuild your product until your passion is complete. Believe in yourself and believe in your dream — and then push, push,

push, and push. Don't let the dream die. The only obstacles are in your own mind. You'll find out more about obstacles in the following chapters and how to overcome them.

Don't second guess your first instinct. If it looks like an opportunity, take it. The reason people fail is because they fail to take action. And it's important to not just take action, but to *finish* the action. You must take all the steps until you've reached the finish line. Realize that not all opportunities are going to make it, but if you don't put them out there and if you don't see them through to completion, you'll never succeed. Many people get caught at the bottom of the bell curve. They think the prospect of opportunity is such a big mountain to climb that they are afraid of taking the risk and the time. That is why less than three percent of the population are multi-millionaires. The rest are too afraid to climb that mountain. Few people take the risks or finish the tasks to get to the next level. All it takes is finishing, so don't stop. Recognize the opportunities and take action. Do what it takes to make your dreams come true.

Looking Forward to Change

Once upon a time I worked for a well-known health insurance provider. I was in management for the Group Medicare Program and sold insurance programs to Fortune 50 companies. It was a hard sell and sometimes deals could take years to close, but when they closed, they were big.

Right about that same time, my employer was merging with another company. At that point I started to see some signs that changes were coming and they were coming quickly. One of the signs, especially on the Individual Medicare side of the business, was that the old way of doing business (going door-to-door and selling one case at a time) was going by the wayside. In fact, they were moving the whole Medicare department down to Louisville. Several top managers were being released — even though their numbers were clearly good.

All divisions of Individual Medicare were being moved except my department, since we handled the large corporations. In hindsight, the signs were clear — this was not something that was going to hold, and someone in the new regime would want to move my department closer to the home office and eliminate other departments.

I started to notice my immediate boss wasn't quite as interested in the new numbers I was bringing in. But I was preoccupied by the fact that a whole new group within the company was interested in me, particularly with my leads and the process I used to obtain business.

For weeks, top management from the new group had been asking me about the process I used and how I had become so successful in this area. I foolishly let myself believe that they were awestruck by my skills and that I might even be promoted to a higher level — maybe even to head up the Medicare area. Much to my surprise, the opposite was true. I was one of the lucky few. I say "lucky" because I got a clear warning; my boss' boss actually came to my office and told me a few months ahead of time that the new company would be moving our department down to Louisville and I had better start looking for a new job.

By this point in my life I had been down-sized, up-sized, right-sized, fired, hired and not hired. I had seen so many changes — and I had learned to be excited when the next one came along! Anytime I left a company, I was so happy I could hardly stand it. Why?

Because I had two choices:

- I could be sad and destructive to myself and others.

- I could be happy and look out at the horizon and see what the next great adventure was going to be.

I chose the latter, every single time. Now, I'm not saying that being laid off didn't hurt and that I didn't go through a period of pain. I'm only human. But I'm saying that I did not sit there and relive what I woulda, coulda, shoulda done until I shoulda'd all over myself! I had already learned how to pick myself up, get out, and make something positive happen. And I kept this positive attitude not just for me, but for the people around me. So many people came up to me and asked, "How can you be so happy despite everything that's going on?" And I would always patiently explain what I knew — that although this situation appeared to be an upheaval in my life, in reality I knew that it merely meant a new opportunity was about to come my way, and wasn't that exciting? I'm pleased to say that my own ability to look for the positive side of things actually helped other people to look on the bright side as well. My upbeat attitude encouraged other people and taught them the importance of optimism.

Here's my lesson: Be prepared for change, because change happens. And that's a good thing!

No matter your current employment situation, if you're considering making the leap into entrepreneurism, you're about to make a huge change. Perhaps the biggest change of your life. It can be scary, I know. Downright terrifying even. But I'm here to tell you, it's okay. You can do this! Accepting this change and embracing it may be the toughest thing you'll ever do, but it will also be the most rewarding moment of your life.

I've found, though, that it's easier to embrace change when you can see it coming. It's when change blind sides us that we lose our nerve.

The other day I spoke with a woman who was still feeling the hurt and the pain of being laid off. She had worked for a bank for 30 years, put her heart and soul into the company, and had moved up the ladder to a senior vice president position. But the bank was sold to another bank, and she was caught in the downsizing. At 53 years of age, she had been looking forward to reaching age 55, at which point she would have earned the company's health insurance policy for the rest of her years after retirement. Ironically, when she was laid off, they gave her a severance package along with COBRA for health insurance that took her all the way to three months short of age 55 — denying her the health plan in retirement that she had worked all those years to get.

How many of you are in this same situation now? You've worked your butt off. You've been raised to work for "the man," assuming that "big brother" will take care of you when the time comes...and then they screw you. Yeah, you heard me right; they screw you out of that one final piece of the puzzle you've worked your whole life for. Well guess what? To hell with them. As an entrepreneur, you'll make more money than you could ever imagine, and you'll be happier than you could ever imagine, once you let go of that sour grape and accept the change. The more you linger on what was, the less you'll be able to see what can be. The resentment will stay in front of you and cloud all your dreams. Yes, go ahead and mourn your loss. Losing a job can be as big of a loss as losing a loved one; you need to mourn. But do it, and move on with your life.

By all means, if you've been let go from a job, thoroughly research whether your employer followed all the legalities of letting you go. After all, you do want to make sure they didn't take advantage of you. Many times we're afraid to ask for what is rightfully ours. If you're 40 years of age or older, there are laws to protect you from being dismissed unfairly. Keep in mind though, that in many states you may be considered an "at will" employee, and your employer may have the right to terminate at any time for any reason, but you can still question the final decision. There are laws on equal rights and equal pay. There are laws to extend your benefits beyond your termination date, such as COBRA for the larger employers and state continuation coverage for smaller employers. If you feel you've been treated unfairly, then pursue the path of justice, but don't make it such a big part of your life that you cannot move forward with your new life. Many people have a hard time letting go of the past. Look toward the future and feel blessed that you're finally out of that job and can move ahead to the next opportunity awaiting you.

Okay, now we're done with that chapter of our lives! Whew — doesn't that feel better? Thank goodness now you don't have to sit around and wait for anyone else to tell you what to do...because it's time to take action with your life.

My choice, of course, is to own my own business. Stop thinking someone else can take care of your life and your family's life better than you can. You're in charge now.

Change is coming, and that's a good thing.

HOW TO RECOGNIZE CHANGE

When I worked for the health insurance company, I might have been better prepared for the change if I had seen it coming. And the woman who was laid off from the bank, had she known the change that was heading her way, she might have been able to start planning for her life after the bank far sooner. We're all capable of embracing change, but it helps if we've got a head start.

So how do we pick up on the signals that change is coming?

Four places to look for change coming your way

1. THE OUTSIDE WORLD. Observe the outside world around you. For example, I had a client who manufactured suitcases. When 9/11 occurred, he contacted me and asked me to change his insurance plan to one that was more affordable. The suitcase market had disappeared overnight because people were not traveling, and he needed to cut expenses.

   When I walked into his office, however, I was surprised at what I saw. All over his desk were patterns and various materials, such as cloth, insulation and plastics. In his hands he held a newly sewn cooler — he was looking at the seams and the materials. He had several of his lead managers doing the same. When I asked what he was doing, he said, "Well, I have the equipment and the knowledge to make any type of bag I want. So I'm choosing coolers!" Now there was a man who looked at this mammoth change, took the bull by the horns and turned it around for himself, his people and his company! This man was well into his 80's and had seen a lot of change over the years. He knew what to do about it and he put his plan into action.

2. **THE COMPETITION.** Watch your competitors — be it a co-worker or another business — and note what they are doing. Are they selling more on the internet? Doing more educational seminars? How are they responding to changing circumstances? Decide if you want to follow how others have dealt with a change, or if you want to be on the cutting edge of the change. Be where you're most comfortable. That mouse trap might already be built, but you may have a twist on it that someone else has not thought of.

   A prime example is Thomas Edison. He wasn't the first one to create an electric light bulb, and throughout his career he faced stiff competition. But Edison took the development further than anyone had at the time. The challenge was to find material for the filament inside the glass bulb that would burn softly enough to light an interior room, and burn long enough to be practical. Edison and his researchers tested over six thousand different materials...until he finally decided to try a carbonized cotton thread filament, and he struck gold. The lesson here? Look at all your options, and when change is in your presence, grab it and work with it until you have created the right formula that will send you leaping in the right direction.

3. **YOUR VENDORS.** Are your vendors sensing a change is in the air? Are they changing staff around? Are there fewer people to help you? Should you be looking at changing vendors?

   A prime example of this for me was within the health insurance industry. When health care reform began, I started to notice a shift in the carriers. Some carriers were getting out of the business altogether, while others were leaning toward not paying any broker commissions or limiting the commissions. They were all anticipating the year 2014, when in all likelihood brokers will no longer be needed in the health insurance market; therefore, the carriers were starting to eliminate that expense now. So watch your vendors and see how they are reacting to changes in your industry. You want to make sure that you have vendors that are looking out for your best interest, and that they know what is going on in your industry. They are usually the ones that will feel the change first due to their base of larger clients who may be shifting their spending, therefore affecting the vendor's bottom line. Change early when you see this occurring.

4. **INSIDE YOUR WORLD.** Personally, have you seen or experienced change in how others are reacting or interacting with you? Notice the changes. It may be that other people are reacting to a change in you. You also may find that as you become more aware of change, you'll attract change to you. You are what you think!

   Begin looking for change. Begin looking for how you can build your business. Who do you need to talk to, what products do you need more information on, what will be your next step to build a strong business now? Look for the change and embrace it. What is your "gut" telling you to do? Follow it!

A lot of folks would prefer to be shell-bound turtles. In fact, sometimes we're all turtles; sometimes all we want is to sit right where we are and do absolutely nothing. We'd like to sit safely inside our shells and let others take charge and make the hard decisions. Well, believe it or not, I understand. Everyone needs some down time; if you don't ever take the time you need to recharge, you won't be successful in creative thought nor will you succeed in making the most of your new change. But once you have had your down time and are refreshed, then it's time to leap frog right over the obstacles and embrace change to its fullest! Don't be afraid to leap over those shell-bound turtles. I assure you, those who don't embrace change will be left behind.

For example, we all can plainly observe the changing of the seasons. But is that change beautiful, or does it actually represent the struggle between life and death? Some might say winter is a negative, as the leaves disappear from the trees and the cold shuts down the outward appearance of life. In reality, I think winter is a positive. As the leaves fall, the trees go into hibernation and restore themselves. If the leaves remained on the trees and did not fall when they were supposed to, then all the water in the trees would evaporate out of the open holes in their leaves, and the trees would die. But nature recognizes the power of change. And so the trees go through their annual metamorphosis, so that in the spring the world is born anew. What a perfect symbol of how letting change take its course can bring about an end result that is ultimately positive!

However, there's an important difference between the changing of the seasons and the changes that you experience in your life. You can control how you respond to the changes that occur in your life. How many times have you been in a situation where you felt you had no control over what was going to happen? Now, you may not have had control over the changes themselves, i.e., the death of a loved one, the closing of the company doors, or the economy going bust. But you do have control over how you handle any particular situation. And more times than not, you have clear signals that change is about to occur...but you either choose to ignore the signs or you don't recognize them as such.

Let's take a look at what signs I missed prior to the BIG change that hit me at the insurance company:

- My company merged with another company

- My company changed how they sold one of their core programs

- A sister division was closed and moved to Louisville

- Upper management was being let go, even if they had been successful in their positions

- My boss wasn't as interested in my numbers

- Outside people wanted to learn about my process and how I built the business

- My boss' boss warned me to look out!

What were my mistakes?

- **NOT TAKING ACTION.** Immediately, I should have started looking for a new position — even if I thought the new company was going to keep me. This might have involved updating my resume, conducting online job searches, starting to network more, talking to recruiters in the area, or even starting my own company. It never hurts to look at all the options!

- **NOT READING BLATANT SIGNS.** Top successful management was being let go — that was a huge sign that I chose not to notice.

Life is simply steps of learning. As we grow, we improve our ability to notice change before it occurs. The more readily we see change coming, the more quickly we can take advantage of the change and act upon it.

I asked my daughter if she had ever been in a situation where a change had occurred and she had been caught off guard and felt that black-out feeling — when you're so blind-sided that you can't believe it's happening to you. She recalled for me a time when she lost a group of friends. But when I asked her if she had noticed any warning signs before she lost this group of friends, she said, "You know, looking back, I think that I had started to pull away first. I think I was starting to feel angst and beginning to disassociate myself from the group." I find it interesting that she didn't mention noticing external signs from the group, but instead that she felt something almost like a premonition from inside her somewhere, that she somehow knew something big was about to happen.

Sometimes we don't actually see the particular change that is going to occur, but instead we can feel it's going to occur based upon the overt actions of others. I say overt because the change is clearly in front of you, but you don't see it.

Change is really one of those buzz words right now. Everyone is talking about it and trying to get used to it. It almost sounds like a new phenomenon, like it's never been done before! I believe this is because things are changing much more rapidly than we're used to seeing, and people are trying to adapt quickly. We all go through change. But what we want to do is embrace change and to have fun with it! We all evolve, every single day — every moment — whether we want to or not. Instead of fighting it, enjoy it and go along for the ride. It's always a good one and an opportunity to expand out of the box.

Remember, timing is everything. Change happens at particular times; you may think you're not ready for a change, but just like everything else on this planet, things happen when they're supposed to — no sooner and no later. When change happens, let it flow. Enjoy the ride and push yourself forward. Understand that as you begin going through the change it will seem foreign. A new thought, a new way of looking at things. Observe, and then open your mind to why this change is happening to you.

I used to have so much difficulty with change. There seemed to be so much uncertainty around change. But once I got used to change, I saw that it's something to look forward to. Every job I have had has been an opportunity for me to grow. Whether I was fired or I let myself move on, each job was a learning experience.

This is why I want to remove the specter of uncertainty for you, so you can enjoy and experience change to its fullest extent and take advantage of change as you begin to grow your business.

HOW DO YOU MAKE CHANGE A POSITIVE EXPERIENCE?

Change. Some people hate it, some people love it.

I happen to love it.

But change isn't just something you have to get used to; to succeed as an entrepreneur, you have to embrace change. You may have come from corporate America, you may have worked in the same profession for a number of years or you may have stayed at home for your family. Maybe you've changed companies but stayed in the same line of business. You may have felt safe...as long as "big brother" had a job for you.

There are two types of change: change that happens to you and change that you make happen. Either type of change involves two components:

- Something happens

- Someone reacts

When change happens or is about to happen, whether the change is a positive or a negative, you have to react. This reaction to the change is what makes the difference for you in that particular situation. Your response could be one of three choices:

- You do nothing — which is in fact a response and a decided strategy.

- You take action and begin to move forward with the change – building on the change and making your own path based upon the changes that are occurring around you.

- You take action and begin to move away from the change — building against the change and making your own path based upon the changes that are occurring around you.

Don't waste time on bitterness

When I was a kid, straight off the farm, I worked for a prominent local manufacturer. My boss had worked for this company since he graduated high school. He had always told me, "The company you work for is like family. Always take care of the company, and they will take care of you." Yeah, well. When he turned 60, "the family" decided to give him a window retirement offer. It was basically take it or leave it for him. And although he took it, I don't think he ever got over it. Afterwards, he told me bitterly to forget everything he had told me about trusting and living for the company. I stayed in touch with him over the years, and he was never the same. He continued to resent the company for letting him go, and he just could not move on with his life.

Don't do this to yourself. The company you work for — or worked for — is a business, plain and simple. They can't afford to have emotions; they have a business to run — just like you do (or will, by the time you finish this book). If the company can find someone younger than you, and at half the price, of course they're going to embrace that change! Accept it for what it is, and move on.

On the other hand, if you're the one who is younger and at half the price, be careful. Learn what you can from the company, and then move into your own business as soon as you can. Don't wait. And above all, don't let yourself get lulled into the false security of working for someone else. The only real security is what you can give yourself!

No matter what has brought you to this position of change — whether it was thrust upon you or whether you came here of your own volition — build your own security, by building a business that reflects everything you've learned in your life. It's amazing what you can see if you only look for it. A pattern has been forming all your life, and you probably never realized it! The simplest thing in your past could have put you on this path. You don't necessarily have to identify what this thing may be, but it's good to know that your strengths, as well as your weaknesses, make the total package called you.

Choose how you respond to change

Keep your eyes open and always be ready and willing to accept change. If the change is adverse, look at how you can make it favorable; in other words, how can you change it from a negative to a positive? There is always an opposing force that could lead to a stronger and better outcome.

One of the biggest lessons I've learned over time is the importance of training your mind to control the immediate reaction to the situation. I always start by identifying the worst thing that could happen. Look at that particular possible situation and try to figure out how that makes you feel. Truthfully, the label of the emotion doesn't matter as much as how you respond to the emotion. For example, look at the word "change". If this is a word you label negatively, then that's what it will become for you. Ask yourself if fear is what you're actually experiencing, and if so, how do you manage this feeling logically, in order to overcome this fear?

We are all creatures of habit. Over time, we have all developed habitual ways of handling and managing change. Our instinctual response may be a fight or flight response — based upon our animal instincts. If the change comes to you as a shock, take it — just like a shock absorber! Take in the immediate information, and then release it and look for ways to use the change in a positive manner.

Once we get over the initial shock of the change, then we can choose our response. This means controlling our emotions and allowing a cool down period before we decide our strategy.

Sometimes time will show us how a change that looked so scary while you were in the middle of it was, in fact, a blessing in disguise. Try to look back on how you handled times of change in your life, and look for the positive side of each situation. Do this enough times, and you'll teach yourself how to replace the negative feelings associated with change with positive ones. The easiest way to do this is to come up with one positive thought that replaces each negative thought, so you can immediately pull it from your memory and replace it. It's kind of like a "search and replace" mode for your brain.

When you see change coming your way, look at it as an opportunity, a fresh seed to be planted in a strong fertile ground that can do nothing but grow in the light that you provide for it. Because of you, the seed will become a seedling.

Have you heard of the 80/20 rule? It's a principle that applies to many aspects of life, including change. In my experience, 20% of people take action when they recognize change is coming. 80% wait to see if it will go away. Don't be in the 80%. Be in front of the pack and make the change before anyone else. If your gut says it's a go — then do it! God has put a change in front of you for a reason. If you want, you can sit there and admire it like a beautiful gem — and do nothing but stare at it and wonder if you should put it on a shelf until you figure out what to do with it. Or you can realize that change has been put in front of you for a reason. You are to take advantage of it and put it into action and not just sit and wait for someone else to nab it off your shelf because they know how to use it. Take action now before you lose it and all the opportunities it brings.

You are the light at the end of the tunnel. You are the change. In fact, you can have anything you want. You can do anything you want. The more you understand change and embrace change, the more you'll expand with the world around you.

My only rule is to make sure that what you're doing is helping others. If that is the case, you'll succeed! That may sound a little preachy, but it's true on several levels:

1. If what you do is helping others, then others will identify with what you're doing and it will be easier for you to grow your business; hopefully what you do will solve a problem or make other people's lives easier in some way.

2. If what you do feels good — if you're giving to others — then you're fulfilling one of the reasons you're on this planet.

3. If what you do fulfills a passion, it just plain feels good. You'll feel free and you'll stay true to yourself!

4. You'll know that you have accomplished something that 80% or more of the population won't do because they are still hiding in their shell!

Once you learn how to harness the power of change, the sky is the limit!

 EXERCISE 1.3

Let's look at how you've handled change in the past and what you can do differently to make change more effective.

Write down a time when change happened to you.

What happened right before the change occurred?

What happened before that?

Before that?

Before that?

Before that?

What could you have done at the first sign of a potential change?

What will you do next time this type of situation occurs?

EXERCISE 1.4

What changes do you see coming in your future — either short- or long-term?

What is going to happen to make this change occur? Are you or is someone or something else driving the change?

How will this change affect you personally? Professionally?

How will this change affect other important people in your life?

What are the stages of the change that will take place and when will they take place? (A best guess is okay.) Who will be responsible for each stage of the change?

Do you see this change as a positive? Write down any possible positive outcomes. For example, if you embrace this change, could it increase your business? Could you learn new skills? What might these skills be able to get for you?

Remember, you are in control and as you shape your reaction to this change, you shape your destiny. The glory is yours!

CHAPTER 2

LAY THE FOUNDATION FOR SUCCESS
Erase Bad Habits

ALMOST EVERY MORNING, I WAKE UP AT 5:06 A.M....and then I fall back to sleep until 7:00 a.m. This is one habit I want to change. I would like to stop sleeping in. I want to wake up at 6 o'clock sharp each morning, so I can take advantage of an extra hour in every day. I'll show you how I plan to make that happen.

Because it's best to start your new venture with a clean slate, let's take a look at eliminating some of your bad habits. That means opening your mind to change and to new habits. You cannot be open to change if you continually do what you have always done, so set yourself up for success, not failure. Change your habits now, before they become problems later.

We will discuss some simple solutions. Note that solutions are always simple; if a solution isn't simple, then it's not the right solution for you. All you need to do is believe and act upon your beliefs. Take action and stick to the plan, and your bad habits will become a thing of the past.

WHAT BAD HABITS ARE HOLDING YOU BACK?

First, we need to understand what a habit is. I know you may want to just jump right into changing those habits, but that won't work until you fully understand why you have habits and what they do for you.

Of course a definition is always helpful, so let's start with Wikipedia:

> **Habits** are routines of behavior that are repeated regularly and tend to occur subconsciously, without one being conscious about them. Habitual behavior often goes unnoticed in persons exhibiting it, because a person doesn't need to engage in self-analysis when undertaking routine tasks. Habituation is an extremely simple form of learning, in which an organism, after a period of exposure to a stimulus, stops responding to that stimulus in varied manners. Habits are sometimes compulsory.

Now if we take apart that definition to understand it better, we see that habits are "subconscious," meaning you don't even have to think about them. A habit may rise to the conscious level every once in a while, but typically it's something you don't even realize you're doing. You've done something time and time again and you continue to do it in the way you always have.

Think about anything you have learned over time. We tend to do the same things day in and day out, and our whole day is made up of habits. Do you have a routine when you get out of bed in the morning? Do you have a routine of driving to work every day following the same path? Are these good habits or bad ones? Now start to think about what you might want to change, or what new habits you might want to create, that will help you in your new business. Read on, and we'll discuss this more.

CAN HABITS BE HELPFUL?

Yes they can. They can help us survive as well as increase our awareness of self.

Actually, habits are a part of our survival instinct. Our survival instincts are created through a habitual way of reacting to particular situations, therefore, protecting us in our time of need. If we had to relearn how to react to danger every time we faced danger, we would not survive. This type of habit-forming behavior is part of our basic instincts which reside in the subconscious until we call them into action.

When you think of a habit, picture a pill capsule. Imagine that every one of the beads in the capsule is any emotion, reaction, action or thought that you have ever had about handling a particular subject. It's your habit capsule! We have built some habits for survival, some for getting out of bed in the morning, and some to make it through the day. Many times these habits become part of our image, our personality. This is where the saying "you can't teach an old dog new tricks" comes from! Our habits become so ingrained they become hard to change. The more we take our habit capsules, the more they become part of us.

What we want to do is focus on those habits that are problems and that may hinder you from starting your own business. Freedom comes from the elimination of habits that stop you from functioning at peak performance. **It's time to replace the** (DINI) **bad with the good.**

THE PHYSIOLOGY OF HABITS

Some people may think habits are easy to change. But if you thought so, you probably wouldn't be reading this chapter!

Did you know that the act of doing something again and again produces physical changes in your brain? Every experience you have — every thought you think, every action you take — impacts your brain. When you do something repetitively, your brain actually rewires itself. Every time you think a thought or perform an action, a neural pathway is formed. As you repeat that thought or action multiple times, the pathway is strengthened, again and again, until the pathway becomes strong and wide. There is a theory that a sheath of myelin eventually encases the neural pathway, which makes the pathway work even faster and strengthens the habit even further. This is why we have to be so careful with the thoughts and actions we take every day; these habits create a physiological change in our brains!

The more we repeat our bad habits, the harder it is to learn good habits, to the point where neither we nor the outside world can see the good within us. Our bad habits become a mask to reality. Our vision becomes blurred, and we begin to see our bad habits as a controlling force in our world — like something out of a bad movie!

THE 5 STAGES OF CHANGING A HABIT

So are you ready for a change? YES!

We're all looking for a "quick fix." But no matter how much we would like to change a habit overnight, it's not going to happen. The quickest way to get there and to keep a positive change in place is to realize that breaking a habit is a process. You performed your bad habit thousands of times to build this huge pathway of neurons, so you've got to rewire this pathway into the positive habit you desire.

I've identified five stages in recognizing and changing a bad habit:

Stage 1: What bad habit?

At this point you don't even know that you've got a bad habit. Have you ever noticed that it's always easier to recognize a bad habit in someone else? Have you ever tried to get that person to change their particular habit? You can talk until you're blue in the face and still they won't make a change. Why? Because they can't see the bad habit for what it is. Perhaps they're holding onto the bad habit tightly because it's become a core part of their identity. But for change to occur, a person must recognize and admit that a particular habit could be harmful — and the person must want to change.

Stage 2: Maybe it's time for a change...

Now you're beginning to recognize that you've got a bad habit you should probably eliminate. You're weighing the positives and negatives of change and deciding whether you do, in fact, want to change.

There are pros and cons to every habit. Habits can give us a rush of endorphins and make us feel good...or they can cause us problems and steer us off track and make us feel ashamed. At this stage of the game, the negative consequences are beginning to raise their heads and make you wonder if this habit is really worth the hassle.

Stage 3: Okay, let's make a plan.

We can talk and talk and talk, but unless we physically and mentally take action, nothing will happen. **So to prove to yourself that you're serious about getting rid of this habit, write down the steps you're going to take to eliminate it.** This is an essential rule of breaking bad habits. Think about the neural pathway that your habit has formed in your brain, and remember that changing the habit will require both a physical and a mental change. This means you need a CONSCIOUS mental stimulation to bring the habit out of your subconscious and into an active mode of change.

In order for you to effectively change your habits, know that you can only tackle one habit at a time. Don't try to change all of them or even two at once. You'll fail. It takes baby steps to change your habits — one step at a time. You can't accomplish everything at once. This is vital!

For example, have you ever decided to start exercising and then put a really big plan into place? Did you say you were going to run a mile and lift weights every day? It's easy to get so excited about the idea of a positive change that you bite off more than you can chew. You start out with such a big plan that there's no way you'll ever accomplish it all. So don't do that to yourself. Take baby steps. If that means exercising for five to ten minutes a day — do it, until you're ready to take the next step and the next and the next. Stick to the plan every single day, and don't skip even one day, especially for the first thirty days. Because you're reinforcing a new habit, you're actually rebuilding those pathways in your brain.

Now, I know what you're going to say. Exercising every day is too hard. Well, doing a little something every day doesn't have to be strenuous. Lift just a few light weights or jog in place for a few minutes. It's not the exercise we're worried about here — it's building the habit that counts.

It's also critical to write down your plan of action and stick to it.

Keep in mind that if you stumble, if you fall, simply dust yourself off and get going again. No one is perfect, so using that as an excuse for not moving forward is unacceptable. This is the difference between winners and losers in the game of life! When you reach your goal, you'll know no higher accomplishment than the feeling of success that you have done it. You have succeeded. Don't stop!

You can also harness the power of positive self-talk to bring the habits you want to change up to the surface. Your own self-talk — that non-stop chatter in your brain — is ultimately what talks you into or out of doing things. **A great exercise to do for the next week is to write down every time you have a negative thought.** You might notice a pattern of negative thoughts that runs through your mind all day long. Identify these patterns and come up with positive self-talk alternatives to eliminate these negative emotions you use to handle particular situations throughout your day. Realize that practice counts. The more you exercise positive self-talk, the more you'll notice the changes you're making toward positive out-comes for your business and your life, and soon you'll be moving forward.

For my own positive self-talk, I like to use a personal mantra. Most days, I run for exercise. When I run, in my head I'm chanting my mantra: "Build my passion; build my strength; make me happier every day." I have many variations on this and other mantras that I use to create a constant reminder to me that success is my only option.

Visualize your end goal. Understand that what you're doing now is a short process and that your bad habit will go away once you have retrained your mind.

And always, always, keep doing what you're doing! Once you make it past the first thirty days, you're that much closer to sticking with your positive decision forever.

Stage 4: But what about those temptations?

Bad habits exist because we've trained the neurons in our brains to respond to certain triggers — temptations in our environment that cause us to subconsciously revert back to our pre-programmed behavior. Triggers are what you see, do, and think that make you want to go back to your old habits. If you don't replace your triggers with strong good habits, you won't change.

These triggers aren't going away any time soon. In fact, more than likely you've already tried to stop this habit in the past and experienced failure when you stumbled onto a trigger. That's very common. Failure typically occurs when a trigger is introduced. Why? Because your new habit wasn't stronger than your old habit. Your new habit must be stronger and more compelling than the old — and your reason for making the change has to be even stronger.

Make sure you understand why it's critical that you change this bad habit. Remember the ultimate goal and commitment you have made to yourself. Eliminate your old way of thinking, and stay true to your new path.

Another common sense option is to avoid triggers whenever you can. Take away as much temptation as possible. If your children or other family members have candy and potato chips in the house, ask them to stop buying the offending items. If that won't work, then recognize the temptation and be aware that you're committed to break this habit.

You could even give yourself a cue when you start to feel tempted. Your cue could be as simple as a snap of your fingers to snap you into reality and make you consciously aware once again of your written decision to change your bad habit.

Maybe your bad habit is preventing you from working on your plan to start your new company. You might subconsciously throw obstacles in front of your goal because you're afraid. Stop, and replace that obstacle with your new, strong commitment to start your company NOW.

Stay positive. Optimism and a positive attitude are essential, even when you fail. Failure is simply the next step in success. Never give up. Giving up is for losers. Getting back on that horse is what makes you the hero.

Stage 5: Don't forget the reward!

Last but not least is your reward — yea!!! Reinforcement means success. Give to yourself a gift or symbol of your success that you will see every day. Remind yourself every day of what that success feels like until you have completely reinforced the positive habit. Now you can move on to eliminating the next bad habit. Remember, one bad habit at a time! Do this every time you develop a new good habit, and soon you'll see physical evidence of the progress you've made. Won't that feel good?

Remember, YOU ARE THE CHANGE. You'll succeed in all that you do. Learn to soar with the eagles and be all that you were put on this planet to be. Life is too short to stay where you are. Break through today!

EXERCISE 2.1

Let's look at the habits you've created over your lifetime, particularly those that you feel might be holding you back from fulfilling your true potential. Write down every habit you would like eliminate.

Next, I want you to add to this list every bad habit that you or someone else recognizes about you. Do you see what I said there? "Bad habits that someone else recognizes about you." Chances are good you're not even cognizant of some of your bad habits; other people may notice things about you that should be brought to the surface to ponder. Go ahead and ask a trusted friend; you may be surprised at some of the things you do that you didn't even realize.

I would like you to choose one bad habit that you would like to change immediately, and let's consider the pros and cons to changing this bad habit. Write down all the reasons why you should keep the habit, and then write down all the reasons why you should change it.

Let's look at all the positives in support of this habit. Close your eyes and breathe them in. See yourself in the habit. Mentally walk yourself through every step of your habit, from beginning to end. Think about why you do what you do. Internalize what you enjoy about it. Taste it, feel the positive effects from this habit in your brain. Imagine yourself interacting with others while you display this bad habit. What positive feedback do you receive? Now picture yourself alone with the bad habit — again, what's the positive feedback here? If you keep this habit, what will happen? Close your eyes and really feel the positive effects of keeping this bad habit. Don't deny it — realize that you obtain positive feedback, whether it's comfort, security, recognition, or escape. A habit, even a bad one, can give you good feelings.

Next, look at all the negative effects of having the bad habit. Close your eyes again and breathe in all the negatives. See how this habit affects you mentally and physically. Look at how it prevents you from obtaining your goals. Look at how it affects the people around you. See yourself interacting with the bad habit. What negative feedback do you get? If you eliminate the habit, what will you get instead? Close your eyes and really feel the hold this bad habit has on you. Don't deny it — recognize that the habit has power. But also realize that you don't need this habit in your life. You can replace it with a positive habit.

Compare those positives and negatives, and commit yourself to really changing this habit, once and for all. Write down on paper your powerful, unshakable reason to get rid of this habit forever.

EXERCISE 2.1 *continued*

Now consider what good habit can you put in place of the bad habit? Make your good habit a simple alternative to the bad habit, so it's easy to replace the bad one with the good one. Close your eyes and picture the positive habit you'll use to replace the negative habit. If you don't have a new habit to replace the old habit, you'll fall right back into the same old pattern. Why? Because the trench of that bad habit has already been built as wide and deep as the Grand Canyon. You must begin filling the trench up with the positive new habit.

Take the negative and physically throw it away. Look at your plan for the positive and fill your trench until it overflows with the positive. Encapsulate everything that has to do with your new GOOD habit. Use the encapsulated good habit every time you think of doing the bad habit.

Don't forget to address those factors that trigger your bad habit, too. Write those triggers down. What are you going to replace this trigger with? Now write down why this replacement is important.

For the next couple of weeks, write down each time you take that bad habit out of your subconscious and consciously replace it with a positive habit or a positive trigger. Let's say you want to eat better. Start small. Don't just cut yourself off from all high-calorie foods — pick just one ungodly indulgence and eliminate it. But really do it. If you're eliminating just one food, I don't mean skip it every once in a while. I mean pretend the food doesn't even exist. So if you like to have a small bag of chips or some chocolate before you go to bed — snap out of it. Get rid of it completely. The chips or the chocolate shouldn't even be in your house! And when you feel that craving for the chips or chocolate, instead, make a statement by replacing that bag of chips or chocolate with something really fantastic. What would snap you out of the craving? Would thinking of the negative consequences help? Or would taking a walk outside give you the kick you need? Whatever it is, step out of the "Craving ZONE" and into the new habit you are forming. Replace the bad with the good. Do it now.

Create a symbol for the old bad habit — for example, I like to use a black pipe cleaner, which reminds me of the negative neural pathway my bad habit has created. Take whatever symbol you choose to represent that habit and carry it with you — in your purse or brief case, taped to your computer, in the center console of your car or in your bathroom so you see it in the morning and at night.

EXERCISE 2.1 *continued*

Put that physical reminder somewhere it can continually remind you of your goal. Changing your habit is all about repetition and consciousness.

Now, replace that black pipe cleaner that symbolized the bad habit with a nice pure white one to resemble the good habit and that fabulous new neural pathway you're building in your brain as a result. Physically throw away the old pipe cleaner and replace it with your strong new white one. Every time you do the new habit — add another white pipe cleaner. If you fall back to the old habit add a black one. Keep track until no black pipe cleaners exist.

As you create and perfect your new habit, use the same process every time. Begin building the neurons into new and better patterns, so they can quickly replace your old habit.

Also, as you continue to deal with this bad habit, remember to break the big task down into smaller, more manageable goals, and keep track of your progress so that you have a reason to succeed.

You can do this!

Eliminate the Fear Factor

I know we would all like to have a perfect foundation on which to start our companies — secure, with lots of money and lots of clients just waiting to come on board. But more times than not, that's not the case. In fact, that's part of the challenge of starting your own business — the challenge of persevering and taking action, even if we're secretly afraid that we don't have everything we need to get started. Overcoming this fear may seem daunting at first, but once you get started, once you get your first client, you'll realize that all the tools you've put into place are working for you. This is why I've devoted this chapter to removing all the obstacles out of your way so that you can focus on what you do best — making money! At this point in the book, you have identified your strengths, your passions and where you're heading. Now let's look at how you can overcome your fears, so that you have a clear path before you leading to success. Let me tell you about someone I met with recently, and let's see what we can learn from his story.

This man has worked in the senior care industry for more than ten years. Along the way, he noticed a gap in the services that his current employer offers to seniors. And he wants to build a business of his own to fill that gap.

This relates to transitional care services, which helps adult children move their parents, when the time is right, into assisted living or other types of care. The company my friend wants to start will manage all the stages and the details of the move, including helping to get the seniors settled into their new homes and sell or get rid of items they don't want. The company will also dispose of belongings when the senior passes away.

Wow — what a powerful business! When we sat down to talk, the first thing he did was rattle off all the things he's done to prepare for the new business. He's built a marketing plan, chosen the name for the company, created a logo, developed a brochure, decided what services to offer, identified his target markets…and the list went on and on. He even mentioned that his wife is a nurse and making good money and would help support their family and two children.

So what's wrong with this picture? He's scared to take the first step.

He's afraid that the first step will push him to the next level that he might not be ready for. He's worried about not being the main bread winner. And he's definitely afraid of failure. He has so much "stuff" running around in his head, he can't move. At his current job, he can't keep his mind on business — every chance he gets he's writing or dreaming about the next steps of his new company. So what should he do?

Some people would say, "Boy, he needs to hire a business coach," or "He needs to build out his plan more." Hogwash. Nobody and nothing can take him to that next step, except for him.

It was interesting to hear him talk about where he's at in his plan right now; he's at the same place I was, many years ago. He just cashed in a $10,000 CD, and on the one hand he wants to move forward, and yet on the other, he's subconsciously looking for the next obstacle to throw into his path so he doesn't have to take that scary first step.

So I asked him, "What's holding you back?" He thought for few minutes and finally said, "There's just so much still to do; I don't know where to start." I told him, "Yes, you do! You can do anything. Just pick something, and start there!" He thought about that for a bit, and then he said that before he could incorporate his business, he needed to do a name search to make sure he could use the company name he'd chosen. I said that was a good start, but I explained to him that he didn't need to have the name picked out and he didn't have to be incorporated before he could start making money. "Just pick your first client and do it," I told him.

He admitted that he already had his first client picked out. His brother-in-law lives down in Texas, and the brother-in-law's mother lives up here in Illinois. She needs to move into senior housing, but the brother-in-law can't take time off to move her and get her settled. I jumped at that. "Great! Do it for him! Now!" He worried that he probably shouldn't charge his brother-in-law — it was family, after all. I told him he had to charge his brother-in-law. After all, he'd be providing a great service for his brother-in-law and free simply isn't an option. The brother-in-law would hire my friend for his expertise, not because he wanted a cheap solution. And besides, there was a bigger picture at stake here; if my friend didn't request payment for this, he wouldn't see this as a true client situation — meaning he'd be back to square one with no benefit and no money.

He said okay, he'd make the move.

"So now," I said, "you have your first client. What else is stopping you?"

"I want my company name to become legal," he said. I suggested he use an attorney to do a full name search for him. This should only cost a few hundred dollars and would be well worth it. Yes, he could do it himself, but with the help of an attorney the search becomes more official.

Also, after the search was complete, he would need to choose whether he would establish his company as an LLC, S-corporation, C-corporation, etc. He said he didn't know how to choose this nor did he know the tax implications. So I gave him the name of my CPA who could walk him through the complete process and help him incorporate his company.

I asked him when he would contact the attorney, and he said "soon." I said that wasn't good enough, but he could not — or would not — give me a solid date. It was as if he wanted to hold onto his obstacles by refusing to make the time to take these steps we had discussed. Well, it so happened that we were sitting in a coffee shop just a block down from my attorney's office, so I suggested we go see my attorney right now. Cell phone in hand, I called my attorney and set up the appointment right then and there. I also called my accountant and set up that appointment as well. No more excuses, no more reasons not to move forward! My friend thanked me and headed out the door and on to his new venture — with two obstacles out of the way.

The morale of the story is, if you can't get past the hows and the whens no matter what you try to do, find someone who will give you a kick in the pants. Don't go for the soft touch; you need a jolt. Let me tell you, once you've done it, you'll be on your way.

WE CREATE OUR OWN FEAR!

I was sitting in Starbucks the other day thinking about how to write this section of the book and how I could make it relevant so that people can learn. I stayed there for a few hours. Next to me were two people talking about their religion, specifically, discussing different ideas to help their church and a boys' soccer team they were forming. They spoke with candor about the boys and the fears they were feeling at this stage in their lives. I found this interesting, since fear was the topic I was about to explore in writing. I pulled out my laptop and began writing about fear, amazed at the coincidence that I was writing about fear and across from me were two people discussing fear.

Soon Starbucks lost its luster and the air conditioning was up just a little too high for my liking. I was having difficulty getting any words on paper. I went out to the car — which for me happens to be one of my best thinking spots. (Since I'm on the road a lot, my car is like my second home. The warm feeling of the leather seats, the view of the world outside through the window with the warm sun coming through, and the familiar smells of my own vehicle lured me into the seat.) I started writing with passion — when all of the sudden the phone rang. It was my husband. I told him of what I had heard and wrote about fear that morning. After our conversation he asked if I would go back in and get some coffee for him.

I went back into Starbucks to place his order, and eventually another comfortable seat beckoned me to sit down and write. There, sitting on a small, well-worn table, someone had left behind a religious pamphlet on fear. Talk about strange forces working in my favor! I actually laughed and cried at the same time (not too loudly of course — since I was in Starbucks!). This is what I call taking action and creating opportunities! Things happen for a reason and are put in your path for a reason. Do not dismiss them. Acknowledge and act on them as I have done here. All of this was a huge breakthrough for me and freed me to write about fear, honestly and from the heart. So let's dive in!

Fear is manufactured from within you. It's not caused by outside forces, but instead it's something that you create.

As we look at our particular situations in life, we try to put a "label" on what we are feeling. And yet it's not the "label" that matters as much as the definition of that label. Is fear really what you're feeling and if so, how can you logically manage this feeling in order to overcome this fear?

One of the most profound discoveries I've made in my life was the understanding that I and I alone am responsible for my destiny in life. As I mentioned in the prologue, deciding to own my own business was a freeing experience for me. But at the same time, it was also unsettling. I realized that no amount of explaining to someone else, no amount of praying, and no amount of wishing would make my dreams become reality. My destiny would only become reality if I did something — if I physically and mentally took action. That discovery was both exciting and terrifying!

There are different levels of fear. There are those fears that have been with us for a lifetime, those that have been with us for a moment, and those that we foresee coming in the future.

The interesting thing about fear is that we own it. Fear is in our minds and ours alone. We build fear based upon our prior experiences. In essence, we create our own suffering — no one does this for us. What frightens us most is the thought of being afraid. But it's an illusion. Our fear produces the illusion of danger. Nothing puts us in more danger than our own mind. There is no protection against fear, and even when we think that we have found safety, we still wonder if our defenses are strong enough, and this uncertainty destroys our security. You must acknowledge the fear and move past it.

Fear is a negative emotion — a delusion — where we set in our minds that something bad will happen, or that we are not good enough to get to the next level in any particular situation. This type of delusion can occur in any type of negative or fearful situation we fabricate.

Have you ever been very fearful of a situation, and once you experienced it, you realized you were afraid for no reason? Probably one of my first fears was of getting fired. I think I was afraid that I wasn't good enough for the company I was working for. I felt small. Eventually I realized that it wasn't that I wasn't good enough; it was simply time for me to leave and find the next level in my life, rather than stay in a job that didn't fit me anymore. It was time that I was confident in my own opinion, my own capabilities, and my own instincts.

Fear exaggerates your limitations, incapacities, quality and potential for growth. Let's look into this further.

FEAR AND SELF-CONFIDENCE

For most of us, fear is simply a lack of self-confidence in a particular area. We may disguise our fear and put up an internal facade to form a delusion instead of recognizing fear for what it truly is. It's our own mind telling us we're not capable.

As an entrepreneur, you'll need a lot of self-confidence. Many people feel they're lacking in this area, but you would be surprised at how much self-confidence you really have, if you know how to recognize it and how to chase away the fear.

I find I can build up my confidence when I can understand what really lies behind my fear. But for a long time, I had trouble identifying why I feared certain things. And of course much of the time, I've simply fabricated the fear in my own mind. Here is an example:

Several years ago, I provided a potential client with information on a health insurance plan she was considering. In this situation, she had a child with a pre-existing condition that she was trying to get covered. (At this point in time, individual health insurance plans provided limited, if any, coverage for pre-existing conditions.) This woman was extremely difficult to work with; she was very demanding and had a tendency to talk over me when I was explaining things to her. I recommended one company over another based on my 25 years of experience in the field; I knew that particular carrier would probably provide more coverage than the other. I also explained to her what she needed to do next. Well, she came back a week later and said she wanted to work with the other carrier. I warned her there could be a problem with coverage due to her child's pre-existing condition. She got extremely angry with me and insisted that wasn't what I told her the first time. I remained calm and listened. After trying to again help her, I soon realized I could not work with her. This was the first time in my life I fired a client. I told her I would find someone else for her to work with, but that I did not feel we were a good match.

In any given week, I might deal with hundreds of clients. As I thought more about this situation, I became worried that perhaps I had told her something incorrectly. I began to doubt myself and what I had told her. I became fearful. I fretted over what could happen. Could she spread bad news about me? Could she ruin my reputation? I turned the situation over and over in my head, until I finally told myself, "STOP!" And I took a step back from the situation. I even called an employee of mine and explained to her what had happened. My employee said, "Sometimes people protest and overreact when they know they are trying to get their way and they cannot. They get mad because they're hoping their anger will push the issue in their favor." I thought about this and realized she was exactly right.

When I went back and reviewed the situation, I was pleased to see that I had taken all the appropriate steps in documenting our conversations and providing accurate information — which proved to myself that I had not lost my mind! Finally I was able to calm down enough to send my ex-client some additional information explaining her options and a recommendation for someone else she could work with. This additional follow-through closed the deal and cleansed away my fear.

Looking back, why did I overreact the first time? I had lost my self-confidence. I doubted my own abilities when I should have trusted my years of experience.

Let's take the concept of self-confidence and analyze it based upon my story. Fear can affect 4 areas of your self-confidence:

COMPETENCE. In the above scenario, rather than trust in my own experience, I immediately doubted how well I knew my subject matter. I cut myself down because I incorrectly believed this woman. I felt like a loser. Incompetent. But what really was the truth in the matter? In reality, I had done everything right. This woman was abusive and needed to work with someone else. Hopefully I at least showed her that people won't tolerate her abuse and that the next time she asks for help, she should stop and listen more carefully before becoming defensive and making wild accusations.

Have you ever been in a situation where fear compromised your ability to trust in your own knowledge and experience? Were you under your own illusion that you weren't good enough or that the information you provided wasn't adequate? Recognize these situations for what they are — and not what you manufacture in your own mind.

WORTH. I believed I had not given her the information she needed. I felt I had let her down — while the truth was I had provided her the correct information, but she didn't like the answer, and so she attacked me instead.

Have you ever felt that the fear you've created in your own mind has diminished your sense of worth or the goodness, usefulness, or importance of what you're doing? Remind yourself that there's a reason why you started this business; you're helping real people solve real problems!

GROWTH. My gut reaction in this above scenario was to shrink away from the situation. I wanted to run and hide and not provide any more information. Let her figure it out! Instead of facing the situation and looking at how I could handle it differently or how I could make this bad situation good, I wanted to run.

Fear can trigger a fight or flight response. Have you ever been in a situation when you're fearful and it's difficult — if not impossible — to move forward in a positive way and to grow to your fullest potential? Fear pulls you back and keeps you from reaching your full capacity for growth.

Don't stop reaching, don't stop learning, and don't stop growing your business!

CONTROL OF THE SITUATION. I had lost control. My own self-doubt put blinders on me and I was looking at the world in another state of mind, fogged by fear and delusion. I needed to snap out of it and find a way to build instead of tear down.

Have you ever lost control of a situation and felt a total loss of self-confidence as a result? When this happens, it's like you're lost in a fog. The loss of control can stop you in your tracks and leave you not knowing which way to turn.

Remember that you're the business owner. You're the expert. YOU can solve this problem, get past this fear, and take back control of the situation. The power is in your hands. Use it!

In order to move past your fear and not let it slow your business down, it helps to **identify how your fear is affecting your self-confidence and eliminate** 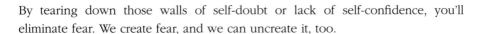 **it**, so you can easily walk in front of any situation, confident that fear will not prevail! Identifying your fear takes away the feeling that you're not in control of the situation. When you understand that you're in total control and no one can take that control away except for you, you'll then create a pattern — a habit — of managing fear by identifying where in your subconscious the fear lies and lessening its power over you.

By tearing down those walls of self-doubt or lack of self-confidence, you'll eliminate fear. We create fear, and we can uncreate it, too.

HOW FEAR MANIFESTS ITSELF IN YOUR EMOTIONS

Many different emotions can serve as masks for fear. Let's take a look at some of them, so that you can see these emotions and the fear behind them for what they really are — and get past them.

GUILT. All of us have felt guilt at some time or another. It's a feeling of having done something wrong, accompanied by shame and regret. Guilt can wrack your self-confidence. When you're afraid and overcome with guilt, do you feel competent, that you have worth, that you can grow or are in control of the situation? Probably not.

EMBARRASSMENT. When someone or something embarrasses you, do you have a tendency to shrink away or to lash out? These are actually common symptoms of fear. How does this embarrassment affect your self-confidence, and how is it stopping you from moving forward and growing in your goals for your business?

ANGER. You can use anger as a tool to circumvent a particular situation. You may even hope that the situation will go away if you get angry enough. Using anger to try to control the situation involves harnessing the power of negative thoughts and actions. Not a good way to do business! It might get you somewhere for a little while, but very quickly you find yourself standing alone.

When someone is angry, many times that anger is a facade for fear. A person becomes angry and lashes out like a cornered animal, in the hopes of making the scary situation go away. But beware; anger can break relationships for a life time. People may lose their trust in you and will not be comfortable interacting with you because they will be afraid of you; they will fear how you overreact to situations and therefore they will distance themselves from you or outright break contact with you. Make sure you understand why you're angry and do whatever it takes to bring yourself back to logic quickly.

 A few extra notes on anger: **When you begin to feel anger boil up inside of you — and let's say you're in a public situation where you cannot or absolutely should not let that emotion be seen** — stop and control yourself. I know this is easier said than done. But allowing that outburst of anger can truly ruin your reputation as a reasonable business person. You'll look like a little kid having a temper tantrum — not a good impression. Getting angry is actually the easy way out. It's an emotion that you can easily let out. Stop the pattern. Step away from the situation if you can, and return to it later when you're thinking more rationally. If you can't do this, then learn to replace your anger with a positive emotion.

Let's say you do let your anger out at someone or something. Later, when things have calmed down, stop and analyze what you could have done differently to make the situation better. Mentally replace the anger you were feeling at the time with an emotion stronger than your anger — such as the realization that you looked immature and unprofessional. Don't ignore the anger or the situation that prompted it; you must deal with it and learn from the situation, not mask it.

 I also find that exercising on a regular basis helps to relieve any pent-up frustration that can easily channel itself into anger. **Exercise is a great stress reliever.** As you get your blood flowing, you'll find that it releases your negative energy. Research different types of exercises, because different approaches work for different people; for some, a very physical boxing class might be a great stress reliever, while others might prefer a relaxing yoga session. Whatever works for you, do it now. Exercise clears the mind and gets you in shape for the next journey in your life!

JEALOUSY. If you're jealous, it's because you lack self-confidence. You have a fear that someone is better than you or that someone will take something away from you. Jealousy can stifle you from moving forward if you think someone else is better than you, because the truth is you'll never be that other person. Instead of worrying about something outside of your control, focus your energy on what makes you great. Focus on what you have to offer instead of mimicking someone who doesn't have the same background and skills you have developed to get you where you're going. You have the better mouse trap and always remember that.

ANXIETY. Anxiety is an emotion that can be positive in the sense that when you're anxious for the next step of a project to occur, that anticipation can actually propel you forward. To be anxious can give you a level of adrenalin that will take you to the next level of success.

On a negative side, anxiety may mean that you're constantly dissatisfied, or it may mean that you're giving yourself a slow heart attack because you're always on edge waiting for whatever is coming around the corner. To be anxious like this can keep you from performing at your top level, because you're always fearful of what's going to happen next. When you focus more on the fear than on what is actually happening, you lose focus and cannot perform as well as you should.

CONQUER FEAR BY TAKING ACTION

I hope I've proved to you that fear is an interpretation of an issue, but it's not the actual issue at hand. Fear can motivate you to take action, prompt a flight response, or it can freeze you so solid you can't move in any direction. But once you overcome the initial shock of a fearful situation, invariably you find you must move in one direction or another.

So let's take your blinders off and move forward. At the end of this chapter I've included exercises to help you identify and eliminate your fears.

But before you do this — I implore you to do this next step —, **identify one** **thing in your life that you've been putting off because of fear**. Whether it's fear of failure, fear of success, fear of the unknown — it doesn't matter. Just pick that one thing. Now —don't spend a lot of time mulling over the "what if's" — simply take one step toward doing something to move past this fear. And no, I don't mean sit down and write out a complete plan of action or spend hours writing or thinking about what you're going to do. I mean do just one thing, right away! Whatever that first step might be, take it now. Pick up that phone, drive to that location, pay that bill (or some portion of it), go to that website, write that one paragraph, and review that contract…Whatever your step might be, take it now. Then…take another small step. No more delays. Do it now!

This will free your mind. You'll begin to understand that it doesn't take a lot to eliminate fear, it just takes YOU! You — moving in a direction, any direction! Action causes a reaction, and that reaction causes a ripple that becomes larger and larger, spreading out toward the positive effect of overriding that fear… until it's gone. You'll be surprised to know that the more you face your fear, the easier it is to eliminate it. So face those fears head on. Research them, even. Understand them.

For instance, many years ago I was afraid of spiders. I overcame this fear by writing a ten-page paper on spiders. As I researched spiders, I began to see their beauty and I came to understand why God put them on this green earth. I also used to be afraid of public speaking. I would stand in front of a crowd, or even in front of one person, and I would lose my concentration and simply could not speak intelligently! I wanted to overcome that fear, so like my fear of spiders, I faced my fear of public speaking head on. I began researching different subject matters, and I then practiced public speaking by standing in front of my staff and training them on these topics. Eventually, with much practice, this experience led me to love public speaking. It also helped me realize that I have a passion for helping others overcome the stumbling blocks that keep them from their own passions.

Overcoming fear is simply a matter of facing it and running it over! Learn about, research and study your fear. Remember, too, that the definition of fear is a lack of self-confidence. I guarantee that any — I repeat — any fear you have in your life someone else has also experienced. Don't run from your fear, but embrace it. You'll find that there is rarely a life or death outcome at stake, so take action now!

Would you be surprised to learn that your fear can motivate you to move forward? Fear can actually be a positive signal that you're about to stretch yourself and move out of your comfort zone, which is a good thing and something you'll need to do as a business owner, frequently. You may be afraid that you can't make enough money to get your business going, or you may fear that your product isn't good enough. This fear can be positive in that it will push you forward to do what you need to do to keep going. It would be great if everyone was motivated by positive energizing forces. But remember, even though fear may seem negative at first, once you start analyzing it, you'll eventually realize your fear was what you needed to get you going in the right direction. Push through that fear and get going! Really try to pinpoint where you need to go to get to the next level, and then move in that direction. Don't worry if it feels like you're trying to reach a moving target; life is unpredictable, so deal with it. Change that fear into a positive emotion through action, and soon you'll see your efforts pay off.

 EXERCISE 2.2

Each time you feel fearful, stop and focus on the real issue. Take a deep breath through your nose — try to make the inhale last for four seconds. Hold the breath for four seconds. And then release the breath through your mouth, and let the exhale last for six seconds. This is a great exercise to settle anxiety.

 EXERCISE 2.3

Write down everything you've ever been afraid of, since the time you were little. Name each fear, and indicate if you've overcome it. Which fears are you most proud of overcoming? Place a star next to those. Now circle the fears you still have, and pick three fears you wish to overcome.

Take a closer look at those fears and write down the worst possible thing that could happen if these particular fears became reality. Think about whether the worst scenarios are really life or death situations, or whether they are consequences that you can deal with.

EXERCISE 2.4

Stay focused on something that is making you afraid right now. Write down exactly what it is. Is it something within your control? If so, write down three actions you can take right now to regain control of the situation.

Now pick one of those actions that you can do right now to eliminate your fear. Write down how you will feel as you take action. Go ahead now and take that step. Don't wait; get yourself out of this fearful state immediately so it does not affect any more of your day.

Write down the time and place that you will take the other two steps you've identified. Stick with your plan and follow-through.

Keep Away From Naysayers!

LET NO ONE RUIN YOUR DREAM

Michelle Garcia is a client of mine who owns Bleeding Heart Bakeries. This cutting edge bakery offers punk rock baked goods with flavors you have never tasted before. I tried a lavender cupcake — and it tasted exactly like lavender! Not only is her business unique, but she is also unique. Michelle is tattooed from head to toe and boasts beautiful bright eyes and an easy smile for everyone she meets. Michelle strives for absolute perfection in all that she does. She's highly creative in her bakery and a smart business woman as well. I have never seen or tasted baked goods as delicious as these. Here is her story about how she's dealt with the naysayers in her life:

> "I had a business before Bleeding Heart Bakery and it failed. I learned a lot from this business. One of the main reasons for the business failure was that I didn't know how to get clients to pay me. I dealt with very large companies that considered the need to pay me on time a moot point since my business was so small. After my company failed, I decided to go back to school and get my bachelor's degree in business. It did help me to understand some of the basics of running my own business.

> When starting my second company, I found that I was my biggest naysayer. And I didn't talk to other people about my business, which

made it even harder. When I decided to start Bleeding Heart Bakery, my first child, Gabrielle, had just been born. Since I now had a baby, people said my new company was just a hobby and that I couldn't be a business owner and a mom too. Little did they know that if you tell me I can't do something, I only push and work harder to prove people wrong. I started my company by selling my bakery goods from a farmers market and soon moved to a store front in Chicago. One of the struggles I had was that my product was organic and at that time, organic products were just emerging and no one understood their benefits. I was three to four years ahead of my time.

My husband Vinny has always been one of my biggest supporters. He said instead of selling my products retail, I should sell them wholesale. I consider myself a working-class person, and I wanted to be able to offer this high-end product to people like me and not price it out of the market for them. We needed to stick to our guns and offer the high-quality organic product we had with little to no money. We started by renting a kitchen. To own a kitchen was very expensive and no bank would lend me money — especially with me looking outside the norm with my body art. After searching for funding for a very long time, I finally found a firm called Accion Chicago. Instead of Accion providing money to me directly, I would pick out certain kitchen items that I needed to get the business started and Accion would fund these items. They were the only company that believed in me. On the day I opened the bakery, I found out I was also pregnant with my second child.

My company has grown to three locations. What I find interesting is even with all the success I have today, the people who were naysayers in the beginning are still the same naysayers now. I realize that no amount of success will ever stop the naysayers. My husband Vinny believes in me and that's what matters most. I work well off of negative energy. If someone says I can't do it, I will. Or if something needs to be fixed, I'll fix it. Both of my parents are doctors; that might have something to do with why I want to fix things.

I just had my third child, and the company continues to grow. I now have partners who previously worked for Lettuce Entertain You Enterprises, Inc. and now own a company called The Fifty/50. We are building out a 180 square-foot area and moving back to our old neighborhood. I drew the space and tables to spec. The Fifty/50 is building out the rest of the area for me.

I am more of a creative person and the business side of my business was sucking the life out of me. Take, for example, doing taxes. I used to do my own taxes and almost got myself into very deep water by doing so. Always hire out taxes and payroll. This is too big of a liability to do wrong. Now, with my new partnership, The Fifty/50 will pick up the business side of the business and I will go back to the creative side where I live and breathe more freely. Since I will not be running the business, I will become more creative and will be able to take the time to build the business to the standards I believe in. I believe if you start your business because of your passion, such as cake decorating, once you start your company and start running your business, you get pulled away from your passion and you are no longer an artist. I am glad this opportunity is bringing me back to the creative side where I am the strongest.

Well, Naysayers, see if you still don't believe! We will now have $3.7 million invested in this new venture with my partners who have obtained private investors. We will become a greener and "hipper" bakery with a lot of organic. I will keep my other three locations and am looking at opening up a gluten-free kitchen so we can do large-scale gluten-free baking. Your opportunities are endless when you get out of your own way and stay away from the naysayers."

What Michelle says is powerful stuff.

ONLY YOU CAN TAKE CONTROL

Many people find entrepreneurship to be risky. In my opinion, working for someone else is much more risky because you're not in control of your own future. As you explore entrepreneurship, you'll find a number of naysayers both near and far from you. If you find yourself surrounded by naysayers, it's best to push past them; they have their own fears that need not be part of what you're doing.

If you don't take the steps toward entrepreneurship now, you'll never be satisfied with yourself and with what you consider the ultimate accomplishment in your life. The naysayers may be part of your life, but they are not your life. They are not you. Only you can make it real. Like I said in the prologue, no one can fully understand what you feel and what you're going to do in this lifetime except you. The world around you is real. The things that happen to you are real. The things that happen to other people are real. But what really influences the outcome of everything around you? You do.

You either choose to accept or deny the outcome of each situation. You also choose to influence or to not influence each situation. What is real is what you make real, based upon your focus. If you're focusing on the positive then you'll see the potential positive outcome in everything you do. If you're focusing on the negative, then this is what you'll see. So many times I hear people blame the economy or blame some other outside influence for what is happening within their own business. They don't know that it's all within their control.

The reality is that you're in control of your own destiny and your own business. If outside influences are affecting your business, then identify them and either change your business model or change your business, but don't use these outside influences as a scapegoat. This becomes an excuse for failure when you should be looking at the positive side and finding ways to change or improve your current situation. Don't give up or blame others. Instead, become more conscious of what is going on around you.

FOCUS ON THE POSITIVE TO SEE THE POSITIVE

You'll be amazed, once you open your eyes and listen to all the positive influences around you, how quickly your business will grow and become the highly prosperous business you always dreamed of.

You can take this to the bank. See beyond what is right in front of you and be the visionary you were meant to be. You're a source for goodness in this world, and you will build your business. **That** is reality.

EXERCISE 2.5

Choose five successful business entrepreneurs that you know and take them out for a cup of coffee. This may sound intimidating, but so many of us want to share our stories and help others, that you'll be surprised by the generosity most entrepreneurs have in common. This can also be a great way to get referrals for your new business! Ask them these six basic questions:

1.   Why did you start your own company?

2.   How did you choose your product/service to sell?

3.   Where did you get the money to start your business?

4.   Were your family and/or friends supportive or did you go it alone?

5.   What do you consider your biggest success?

6.   Where do you want to be 5 years from now?

 EXERCISE 2.6

Now go to your favorite coffee house and have a seat. Gather paper and pencil (or computer) and ask yourself these same questions. WAIT! You don't have a business. Yes that's true. Part of succeeding is putting yourself in the mindset of those who succeed. Visualize what your answers will be once you start your own business. What will be the ideal answers for your success?

TARGET YOUR MARKET
BASED UPON YOUR VALUE
Know Your Value Proposition

WHEN YOU'RE SELLING SOMETHING, IT'S IMPORTANT TO KNOW why people will buy from you. What makes your product or service unique? What makes your business unique? Why will people choose you over your competition? This is called your "value proposition." And once you understand your value proposition, you'll be able to explain your products and services to your clients with a clear and persuasive message that will really hit home and get more clients interested in you.

Beth Carter is the founder of Freelance Writing Solutions, and she's also my editor. She helps businesses write compelling marketing materials, and she has this to say about creating your value proposition:

"When I started out in business, my first job was selling credit insurance. This is a product that lets businesses insure their accounts receivables, so that if a customer defaults on an invoice, the insurance company pays the invoice instead — so the business gets paid, no matter what. This isn't like other types of insurance; it's more like a financial product than a typical insurance product. It can get fairly complicated, and so before I felt comfortable selling this to businesses, I learned everything I could about the product. And I mean everything. I learned all the features of credit insurance, inside and out.

Then, when I would go on a sales call and get in front of a potential client, I'd relay all these features to the client. I'd tell them that the insurance does this and it does this and it does this too…and then I'd sit back and wait for the client to "get it." And I'd honestly be surprised at the number of people who just didn't "get it!" Which I find really funny now, because in reality, I didn't get it at all.

My mistake was that I was only talking about my product and the features of my product. I wasn't putting any of this into language that my clients could understand. I wasn't helping them connect the dots between what the product can do *and why that would be important to the client.* I wasn't helping the client make an emotional connection with my product. I was only talking about my product; I wasn't talking about my client at all.

Here's a sample of how I would start out my conversations with clients:
'Your receivables are one of your largest and most at-risk assets. Credit insurance protects against potential bad debt losses, thus providing a safety net for you.'

Yawn.

I mean, I guess it was fine. It was factually correct. But it wasn't inspiring or exciting, and it certainly didn't say much to the client about the difference this credit insurance could actually make to their business.

Now what if I said this to the client instead:
'Imagine knowing that every time you extended credit terms to a buyer, your organization was guaranteed to receive payment. What difference would that confidence make to your sales team?'

Do you see the difference there? I still let the client understand the fundamental aspect of how the credit insurance works, but I put it all into language that revolves around the client, not the product.

This principle is at the heart of figuring out your value proposition. It's a truth of human nature that everyone really only cares about themselves. Clients really don't care about you or your company or your product. All they care about is that they have a problem and they need to fix the problem, and they think your product or service might do just that. Bottom line, that's the ONLY thing that your customers care about. They may like you, they may like your company, but actually, they only really care about their problems. So it is absolutely vital that you are able to express what you do, **from the perspective of your customer**. That's what makes a terrific value proposition that your customers will respond to.

Start by describing what your company does or what your products or services do. Make this purely factual; don't worry about putting any spin on it. Now, ask yourself a critical question: 'Why does this matter to my clients?' Figure out the answer. And ask the question again, of the answer you just came up with: 'Why does this matter to my clients?' Keep answering and asking, until you come up with the very deep, fundamental reason why people buy from you.

Now you've got an outstanding value proposition that should form the basis for every marketing material you create.

For example, going back to my credit insurance days, what does credit insurance do? Well, it protects an accounts receivable from the risk of non-payment. Why does this matter to my clients? Well, the insurance will give them confidence and peace of mind that they're going to be paid, no matter what. Why does this matter to my clients? Well, maybe they'll be more willing to extend attractive payment terms to clients, whereas before they might have been more conservative with their terms. Why does this matter to my clients? Well, maybe these attractive payment terms will help my clients be more competitive in the market place and get more sales. Why does this matter to my clients? Well, more sales means they can grow their company more easily, with less risk. Aha! Now we're getting somewhere!

So when I was selling credit insurance, my value proposition probably should have been something like this:

'I sell credit insurance that guarantees payment on accounts receivables, so that you can confidently extend attractive terms to your buyers, improve your position in the marketplace, and grow your company — risk-free.'

With this value proposition, I've explained what credit insurance does, but I've taken it a step further and connected the dots for the client so that the client understands, right up front, what's in it for him.

Do this with every piece of your marketing. Ask yourself of every statement you make, 'Why does this matter to my clients?' and I guarantee, your marketing will be stronger for it. You'll get the attention of your clients and your marketing will get you the results you want — more sales."

Great advice, Beth!

It's also important to understand that people purchase products or services for three basic reasons:

- To solve problems

- To eliminate pain

- To make themselves feel good

You need to determine which of these categories your product or service is designed to target and then hone in on that target accordingly. You may feel tremendous passion for your product or your company, but your customers only care about what's in it for them. Identify what's in it for your customers, and then let them know!

So let's get you started toward creating your value proposition with a few exercises.

 EXERCISE 3.1

Ask yourself:

- What makes your company unique? List ten unique qualities that no one else or very few other companies offer.

- Why is this important to your clients? List ten reasons.

- Why will people buy your product or service? Will it solve a problem, eliminate pain, or make the user feel good?

- Now put it all together. What do you have that they don't?

Yes, I know this is a very simple exercise, but that is what it's all about. When you boil your brand identity down to the basics, and you put it in the perspective of your clients, you're determining what you and your company have that make you stand out in the crowd. You not only want to identify these unique features, you also want to continually point them out in your presentations, your website and every bit of marketing you do.

Identify Your Clients

WHO ARE YOUR CLIENTS?

Most prospective customers won't know your company or won't be able to tell the difference between your company and others. It's your job to identify your best potential customers and to target your marketing to them. The first step to identifying potential customers is to research them.

Go online and find the most recent edition of the Country and City Data Book, (DINI) published by the U.S. Department of Commerce (you can find it by searching on Google). This tool will give you the most recent census data on specific geographic areas.

The great information this census data gives us leads us to the big question, "Who is your client?" ANYBODY! EVERYBODY! No, not really. You need to look at your opportunities and decide where you want to spend your time. You may find many potential markets, but which ones will be the most profitable? Which will bring you residual income or opportunities to add more products to sell? Since you may have limited resources and limited time, you'll want to use them wisely. Let's focus on what really counts, which means understanding our markets more clearly.

The most successful small businesses understand that only a specific group of people will buy their product or service. The task then is determining, as closely as possible, exactly who those people are and targeting your marketing efforts and dollars towards them. You too can build a better, stronger business, by identifying and serving a particular customer group — your target market.

If you have competition, all the better! This means the client is either already using a similar product or they're thinking about it, which sets the stage for you to come in with the right offer at the right time. Let's face it; there is a market for everything. Do you remember pet rocks? Proof right there!

CAN YOU SEGMENT THESE BUYERS?

Zero in on your target market by using market segmentation. In other words, create "groups" of buyers who all share certain characteristics. Depending on what you're selling, you may be able to create several segments of buyers. **Can you** (DINI) **group your typical clients according to any of these examples listed below?**

- Local

- International

- Government (If this segment applies to you, you may want to look into becoming "certified" as a small business or other certification to give you an advantage in this market.)

- Age: children, teens, young, middle, elderly

- Gender: male, female

- Education: high school, college, university

- Income: low, medium, high

- Marital status: single, married, divorced

- Ethnic and/or religious background

- Family life cycle: newly married, married for 10–20 years, with or without children.

If you're selling to businesses, your segments might go according to industry or company size, but you get the picture. The more details you can identify about your buyers, the better.

Next, see if you can segment your buyers even further, according to behavior styles:

- Lifestyle: conservative, exciting, trendy, economical

- Social class: lower, middle, upper

- Opinion: easily led, highly opinionated, conservative, liberal

- Activities and interests: sports, physical fitness, shopping, books

- Environmentalist

By now a picture should be emerging of who you think your ideal customers are...or who you want them to be. Depending on the nature of your business, you might even be able to write a description of your customers. For example, you might state:

> "My target customer is a middle-class male in his 30's or 40's who is married, has children, is environmentally conscious and physically fit."

Based on your research, you may even know that there are approximately 9,000 of those potential customers in your town! It may well be that 3,000 of them are already loyal to a competitor, but that still leaves 6,000 who are not, or who have not yet purchased the product from anyone. And really, how loyal are those

3,000? Since they've already bought a product similar to yours, they could be an even easier market to target because they already know what to expect, and your unique feature could very easily prompt them to switch to your product or service.

Or your target market could be the top 50 companies in the United States. Or the top 50 banks in your area. Or grocery stores. Whatever — the point is to do the research!

WORK SMART, NOT HARD

By carefully identifying and segmenting your marketplace, you'll find that you've saved yourself a lot of time and effort. We all know there are only so many buyers out there, so we want to increase not only the number of leads we get but, more importantly, our closing ratio too. As a business owner, you want to work smart, not hard.

That doesn't mean not taking action; it means you have to take action in the right direction. And follow-through is crucial. This is one of people's biggest problems — and it's actually associated with fear. People will begin to take an action, but they won't follow through. Just like the terrible "woulda, coulda, shoulda", people will chalk up their inaction to "I'm just lazy," "I ran out of time," "It will never work," or even "Someone told me it would never work." Stop covering up your own fear and insecurities! Move forward and stop "chalking it up!"

Leverage the Internet

BUILD YOUR WEBSITE

I asked a friend of mine, Lori Zoss Kraska, to provide her expertise regarding how entrepreneurs can leverage the power of the internet to grow their businesses. She happens to be a digital marketing professional and Adjunct Professor at Baldwin – Wallace College, so I thought she would have some good advice. Here's what she has to say:

> "The internet is a wonderful source for start-up entrepreneurs as well as for those thinking about expanding a business. Whether you're looking for information about your target market or searching the competition, there are many resources available to aid you during the process.
>
> **If you're looking to start a small- to medium-sized business, a great place to start is the website of the Small Business Administration: www. SBA.gov**. This website is a valuable resource that includes tips for starting a business, government grant information, a local SBA resource directory,

and much more. It also features articles on borrowing money, small business regulation, and business plan development.

Maybe you're looking to gather additional information about various industries and potential competitors. In that case, try **www.Hoovers.com**. The Hoovers website contains information on over 65 million companies, 85 million people and 700 industries. There are many free sections of Hoovers, although the company does charge a subscription fee if you want to access more in-depth information and conduct more specific searches within the site.

 After performing your research online, **don't forget to establish your own online presence with a website**. Building a website is key to your success! Websites are almost required these days to tell your company's story, feature your products and services, interact with your customers and, if applicable, set up an online store. Many people think that it's hard to start a website when in actuality it's simpler than you think. Just type 'build your own website' into your favorite search engine and browse through the hundreds of links to the do-it-yourself site builders that will walk you through the whole process of creating a website. Some of these services offer free- or low-cost hosting for your newly created website, too. Additionally, many do-it-yourself site builders offer marketing packages that help to promote your business online.

One tip when considering site builder packages is the type of reporting and analytics the package provides to its users. At the very least, you'll want a reporting/analytics package that gives you instant access to all the statistics about your website, including the number of people who visit your website, what pages they visit, how long they stay on your site, and where these visitors come from. You'll also want a site builder that offers online and phone technical support 24 hours a day, 7 days a week, in the event you experience any technical problems during the build of your website or after it goes live.

Once you've established your business and have created your official company website, you might want to take advantage of search engine marketing (SEM) tools like Google AdWords to instantly drive customers and prospects to your website. For just dollars a day in some cases, you can begin advertising on the search engines. This is called a 'pay per click' campaign (or 'cost per click' — same thing); in a PPC campaign, your ad appears on Google every time someone types in keywords that you've selected, and you pay a fee every time someone clicks on your ad and goes to your website. For instance, if you're starting a business selling tuna fish sandwiches in Chicago, Illinois and you created a Google AdWords campaign for your site, you might choose to have your ad appear when someone searches for 'tuna fish sandwiches Chicago, Il.' Google does a good job of providing easy-to-use tutorials that walk you through how to start and manage your AdWords campaign. For more information, visit **http://www.google.com/adwords/tutorial.html**.

Finally, as your website traffic and transactions grow, you may want to consider creating a mobile-friendly version of your website. Your big, beautiful website might not display correctly on a small cell phone screen, which is growing in importance as more and more people use their phones to search the web. Some site builders may provide this option, but if yours doesn't, do a Google search for 'mobile ready website templates.' You'll find a list of links to providers who do offer this option."

Thank you, Lori. Great advice for all of us, whether we're new to this technology or not!

TAKE ADVANTAGE OF SOCIAL MEDIA

One thing is clear: the internet has completely changed the way businesses can market themselves. Websites let you reach your audience 24 hours a day, 7 days a week. PPC campaigns let you focus your message on highly targeted audiences. And now social media has opened the market even further.

My friend J.D. Gershbein likes to call this "The Age of the Digital Entrepreneur." J.D. is CEO of Owlish Communications, which helps firms use social media to build their brands and to generate revenue. He compares the impact that social media has had on communication to the impact the airplane had on travel so many years ago — major changes, no doubt, but all for the good!

I asked J.D. how entrepreneurs can use this new phenomenon to grow their businesses, and he immediately recognized the elephant in the room — the truth that for many of us, social media pushes us completely outside of our comfort zones. But the reality is that social media gives us tremendous opportunities to communicate with people; the benefits are simply too great to ignore.

Take LinkedIn, for example. "We do business with those we know, like and trust. LinkedIn can get us to that point at warp speed," J.D. said. He explained that

LinkedIn allows users to create detailed profiles that can be optimized for search engines, which increases a business owner's chance of being found by the right person. A well-written profile will add to your credibility, which can impact your brand and generate momentum. In addition to helping you get found, LinkedIn also makes it very easy for you to do the finding as well. As J.D. stated, "A few simple skills, paired with insightful, strategic messaging, can put the entrepreneur literally right in front of the people who control the purse strings."

J.D. also recommends entrepreneurs utilize Facebook in their campaigns. "The public relations potential of a Facebook business page cannot be underestimated," he said. "Facebook personalizes the venture and lends a sense of humanity to the content. Photos and videos can heighten relevance, create a unique look, and relax the conversation."

"Twitter," J.D. added, "lends itself well to integration with all the online marketing options. It allows for stream of consciousness and focused messaging that can drive traffic and enhance the visibility of the business."

In the end, J.D. believes that success with social media comes down to understanding and using all of the tools available to you. "The digital entrepreneur embraces all available social media platforms and draws a sense of power from using them," he said. "Self-representation is different on each, yet all activities come under the general heading of relationship marketing and involve shaping the perception of mutual benefit. Those that have taken the leap of faith with social are interacting on a more meaningful level. The exchange that takes place on these sites varies widely, but it can make a lasting difference in how business gets done."

I love his use of the phrase "relationship marketing," because that's exactly what successful entrepreneurs do — we work hard to develop meaningful, long-lasting relationships with our customers, in every aspect of our business.

Social Media has taken a more expansive role in marketing, communicating, and growing your business. Changes occur quite frequently in the Social Media platforms, so it takes some knowledge and time to stay up on the latest. It will take time to establish your presence on them. As you know though, the rewards can be very beneficial to your business. Not to be redundant, but Social Media is consistent marketing, it's easy and it's free. Did I mention FREE — yes — what better way to get the word out and save money!

I have a blog at **www.hollykatko.com**, which is also used to provide information to share with our clients and readers. When blogging, there should be blog entries at least a minimum of once per week, although you can add entries daily if the information is pertinent and beneficial to your readers. The blog can also be used to promote any services or products. There should be a link for readers to subscribe to your blog via an RSS Feed. We also provide a monthly newsletter which is emailed to our clients containing specific information on our company and related topics. This is a great FREE benefit for your clients as well as another way to promote your business.

The main Social Networks we use are Facebook, LinkedIn, Twitter, and YouTube. Facebook has Pages which can be set up to have your company name as the title. It can be designed quite extensively, although that will require a learning curve. It can be designed to be very effective and active for your business with frequent posts to let the world know what your business is doing. It can have business to consumer as well as business to business benefits.

Twitter is a constant post waiting to happen. Tweets can be sent to communicate with all consumers or message them directly. This platform is also great to dispense info about what your business or you are up to in the moment and to share knowledge.

LinkedIn is primarily a Business to Business platform. There is the ability to have a personal profile and a company page. Go to an expert like J.D. to find out more.

YouTube is a great searchable tool to post videos about your business or what you are doing. These videos should be posted to your website or linked to from your website. The videos can also be utilized on the other Social Media platforms. Use videos in your newsletters — it's a great way to spread the word! Get yourself a YouTube Channel for an even stronger YouTube presence.

This is a very brief description of Social Media, but you cannot underestimate the importance. There are volumes of very helpful information available on this subject. But, *and this is an enormous but,* you still need to focus on the primary goal of starting your own business, putting all the foundational blocks in place, and then utilizing the benefits of the Social Media platforms.

There is an ever evolving world of Social Media with new facets emerging as this is being written. One of the best ways to learn is to go to each Social Media website and consume the knowledge.

Create your accounts and just get going!

Improve Your Networking Skills

You attract what you are. Put out positive energy, and it will come back to you.

For example, maybe you have a teenage daughter who is studying to become a nurse. Let's say she is planning to attend to the University of Iowa. She wants to get a job in the medical field while she's in college, but no one will hire her because she has no experience, and she's asked you for help. The next week you attend a networking event, where you just so happen to meet the head of a major hospital in your local area. And she just so happens to know of an entry-level position that would be perfect for your daughter! Voila! You have now checked off one of your goals, and you've helped both the hospital administrator and your daughter, all because you got out of bed this morning, got out of your house, got out of your car...and talked to someone! Yes, you took the challenge and you succeeded. (By the way, that was my daughter I was talking about there!)

If you're going to grow your business, you're going to have to get out there and meet people. For many of us, that's a scary proposition. But don't worry. I'm going to give you some fool-proof tools to improve your networking skills and get the most return out of your efforts.

GET OUT OF YOUR CAVE

Let's say you get an invitation in the mail and it looks very important. It's for one of the biggest events of the year, and you know there will be a lot of opportunities for developing high-level contacts and for increasing your exposure to many potential new clients. But you won't know a soul at the event and you've never been to this location before. What do you do?

Throw away the invitation?

Answer it immediately?

Answer it immediately with the intention of not really going?

Let it sit there and hope it goes away?

Run for cover???

When it comes to networking, there are so many roadblocks that can get in your way — right from the very moment you hear about a networking opportunity. If you want, you can make those roadblocks so big that you can't even fathom going to this event. Let's remove them instead. I want you to walk through any door with confidence, knowing exactly what you're going to say and to whom.

First, we have to get you out of your home — your "cave." It's probably the one place you feel safe and secure. It has all the things in it you cherish. It's your space, where you can do what you want. You can sit in front of the fireplace, read a good book or just hide under the blankets being a little afraid, because you don't know who you're going to meet, you don't know what you're going to say and maybe no one will talk to you. But if you stay under the blanket, how will you get your message out to everyone?

Well, let's say you manage to get yourself out of the cave, get in your car and drive to the event. Instead of anticipating a great time and an opportunity to learn from others and share stories, you're more focused on walking in and not knowing a soul. You're afraid that when you walk through the door everyone will stare at you. You might even find yourself slowing the car down or circling the block, or even just sitting in your car in the parking lot not wanting to get out and take those first steps through the door. You'll probably start thinking about all the other things you could be doing right now, and you really don't want to do this and you feel the dread setting in. Have you ever felt this?

Stop and look at what's going through your mind at this moment. Is it fear? If so, cut it off in its tracks. Don't sabotage your success by telling yourself, "No one will like me. I can't talk to people. I'm too embarrassed." Remember in the fear chapter we identified fear and dealt with it. Reread that chapter! Lack of self-confidence and negative self-talk are two of the biggest issues when it comes to fear of networking. But guess what? Sometimes all it takes is a simple change in your self-talk message to give you a new attitude.

Let's replace these negative thoughts with the positive ones now:

Negative: I've always had trouble meeting new people; it's just the way I am.

Positive: I'm having fun meeting new people and I'm getting better at it all the time.

Negative: I don't like to make small talk.

Positive: Small talk is a great way to meet new people; it opens doors to stronger conversations.

Negative: I don't have anything interesting to say; better to keep quiet and look cool.

Positive: I want to extend myself to other people, and I know the best way is to talk to people.

Negative: All these people are busy and don't have time to listen to me.

Positive: These people would learn from me if I provide information to them.

Can you see the difference in the positive versions? Can you feel how empowering they are?

EXERCISE 3.2

Now let's see if you can turn the following negative attitudes about networking into positive statements:

Negative: I have absolutely no desire to walk through those doors and make conversation with anyone.

Positive: _____

Negative: It's going to be the same people with the same conversations. I don't want to go.

Positive: _____

Negative: That group over there looks interesting, but I don't think they would let me in.

Positive: _____

Now you write the negative and the positive statements:

Negative: _____

Positive: _____

Negative: _____

Positive: _____

Another way to look at this is to imagine how it would feel if you said these **negative statements to someone else.** You'd feel obnoxious, rude, etc., right? So treat yourself with the same respect that you would treat someone else! Say and use your positive statements today. Practice positive thinking. You'll enjoy it!

BE WHERE YOUR TARGET MARKET IS

You cannot network effectively without knowing your target market. That's why we addressed targeting your market first. Our time is so limited that ineffective use of our time isn't an option. And yet it's incredibly easy to waste time networking with groups that just don't improve your access to your target market. For example, you might decide to join the local chamber of commerce, where most of the members are small businesses just like yours. But what if your target market is large national companies? In this case, the chamber might help you reach some personal goals, but probably not your business goals. Why spend the money on chamber dues when you could join an industry association where you'll be more likely to find the clients you want?

You attract what you are. If you spend all your time networking with a particular group, then those are the only clients you'll attract. In order to move forward, you have to focus completely on the markets you need — now!

Don't bother with groups that don't put you in front of your target market; drop out of any ineffective groups, even if you've paid for them. Trust me, your time is worth more!

KNOW YOUR GOALS

Have you ever gone to an event hoping that you'll meet someone who will want to do business with you? You dart around the room, moving from person to person, telling them all about what you do and what you sell. By the end of the night you're exhausted and you have nothing to show for it. Or maybe you went to the event and only hung around people you already know because that was your soft cozy blanket, and you closed off your circle to everyone else.

In both situations you've made an effort. You got out of your cave and out of your car, but you didn't network **with purpose**. You have to know *why* you're networking in order to get the results you want.

So why do you go to a networking event? If you say you're there to sell a particular product or service, you're partially right. But another reason you're there might be because you're looking for like-minded people who understand you and your purpose in life.

What is your purpose in life? This purpose becomes part of everything you do, even in networking. Networking with purpose is what it's all about, whether it's for work or for your personal life. So let's identify what your purpose should be when you network.

 EXERCISE 3.3

Let's start by asking a really big question: What is your purpose in life? Write down a goal you would like to obtain in each of the following categories:

Family:

Business:

Financial:

Spiritual:

Self:

Check each area where your networking helps you meet your goals. Identify how your networking is helping you meet these goals, and what type of people you're connecting with to help you meet these goals. Remember, networking isn't only about your business; it can be a great tool for improving your personal life as well. Across all aspects of your life, you have certain goals you're looking forward to achieving. You'll reach these goals much more quickly with the help of others.

As you walk into any networking event, remind yourself why you are there. Keep in the front of your mind:

- What you want to accomplish

- Who you want to talk to

- Why it's important for you to be there

- What you have to give

Then expect the best, because you'll get it!

BODY LANGUAGE

What I love about networking is that you're right in front of a person, so you can easily pick up on cues as you're speaking with them. You can see, hear and feel what's going on as you're connecting with this individual. Knowing how to use this real-time feedback will help you become a better networker.

Handshakes

One of the ways we communicate is through touch — the ubiquitous handshake. I need to point out that the handshake is one of the most important aspects of any face-to-face communication. Without a proper handshake, you lose credibility before you even say a word. Your handshake is critical. What's in a handshake? All the energy from that other person! A handshake can tell you if you're dealing with someone who is:

- Strong

- Weak

- Glad

- Confident

- Fearful

- Reluctant

- Not interested

There are many types of handshakes. Maybe you've experienced a few of these?

The **"half" handshake.** This might signify that the person:

- Doesn't trust you

- Considers you in a different class than themselves

- Treats men and women differently

- Fears getting too close

How does the **half handshake** make you feel?

- That you don't trust the person

- That you've been pushed away before you've even had a chance

The **"wimpy" handshake**. This might signify that the person:

- Is afraid of hurting you

- Doesn't like to be touched

- Doesn't see their handshake as an extension of themselves

- Has been taught to be passive

- Doesn't want to be rude

How does the **wimpy handshake** make you feel?

- That the other person is a pushover

- That you can't take the person seriously

- That you have to drag the conversation out of the person

- That the person has no self-confidence

- That the person is not a hard worker

- That the person isn't putting any effort into talking with you

- That the person simply isn't focused

The **"too-hard" handshake**. This might signify that the person:

- Is trying very hard to make a good first impression

- Wants to show that they are confident

- Wants to show their power

- Thinks more is better

How does the **too-hard handshake** make you feel?

- Uncomfortable and maybe even painful!

- That the person is trying too hard to impress you

- That the person might talk your head off

The **"hand-over-hand" handshake.** This might signify that the person:

- Is trying to show they really care

- Wants to show they mean what they say

- Is trying to outclass you

How does the **hand-over-hand handshake** make you feel?

- That it's inappropriate

- That the person is treating you like a pity case

The **"firm" handshake**. This might signify that the person:

- Knows what they are doing and why they are there

- Is confident

- Is ready to hear what you have to say

- Is there for you

How does the **firm handshake** make you feel?

- Confident in the other person

- Ready to hear what they have to say

Always give a good, firm handshake. Practice if you need to. It's that important.

Eye contact

Eyes are the windows to the soul. They tell you what you need to know about a person very quickly. Direct eye contact is the best approach to take in business, even if you're not comfortable with it. Why? Because 95% of the population communicates through their eyes, not through touch or hearing.

And yet, the next time you're in a networking situation, pay attention to how many people are constantly looking around instead of being focused on their conversation partners. Very few people are good at making direct eye contact. But avoiding eye contact isn't just rude, it's memorable as well…because trust me, people will remember. When people do this to me, I avoid them the next time I see them. Don't be someone others want to avoid. You never know when you'll miss an opportunity to talk with someone who has a client for you!

Here are three simple tips to help you make direct eye contact:

- Keep focused on the person.

- Don't be concerned by what other people in the room are doing.

- Make the person you're talking to feel like they are the only one in the room.

Once you begin a conversation, you must follow through. If you let your eyes roam repeatedly from the person with whom you're speaking, you'll lose all credibility. You'll be remembered as someone who doesn't care, and you'll be remembered as the person not to talk to next time.

Smile

Make sure your smile is genuine and comes with ease. Don't force it. Always be curious about the person with whom you're speaking, and show this through as you're conversing. Let the warmth of the other person be reflected in your smile!

GATHERING YOUR NERVE

Now you're ready to make it happen. Before I begin networking, before I even walk through the door, I like to give myself a little boost when I'm still in my car. I use my own little version of Jabez's prayer and say to myself:

"Oh bless me, Lord, bless me indeed and enlarge my territory. Place your hand upon me. Keep me from evil. Keep me from causing pain."

With the words "Oh bless me, Lord, bless me indeed and enlarge my territory," I'm reminding myself that I want to open my mind to meeting different types of people and different types of opportunities, so when I walk through that door I'm completely ready to take in whatever will come my way. I prepare my mind for success; therefore, I will have success.

With the words "Place your hand upon me," I remind myself that I will have an opportunity to give back today. Whomever I meet, I want to think of ways to help them, think of ways to find customers for them, think of whom else I know in the room that would be a good introduction for this person, because the more I give the more I will get.

With the words "Keep me from evil," I remind myself that not everyone is a positive person, which helps me identify negative influences more quickly. It also reminds me to tap into my past experiences to guide me as well.

And with the final words "Keep me from causing pain," this reminds me that every single person I talk to has been put in front of me for a reason, and if I can help them in any way, I will. That's my job!

Finally, I'm ready to walk in the door. I know my goals, and I've mustered my self-confidence. Uh-oh — but now I have to actually talk to people! Not to worry, it's actually quite simple. Read on to find out more.

CONVERSATIONAL STRATEGIES

High gain questions

Starting conversations is a whole lot easier when you have a list of questions at the ready. These "high gain questions" allow you to get into meaningful conversations at networking events more quickly and with more skill. I go into a lot more detail about high gain questions in the next section of this chapter, but here's a quick introduction to get you started.

First, ask the person a few questions:

Motive: Why is the person there? Start at the beginning.

Advantage: What does the person do? How does he or she help customers?

Probe: What else can you learn about the person? (Use your High Gain Questions)

Next, deliver your capabilities statement, which should include:

Your name and company name — plus your title to lend credibility

Own product — what does your company do and who are your clients

Unique benefit that you offer your clients

Your high gain questions will help you network more efficiently. You'll want to practice these before you go into the networking group so you can effortlessly converse with your next new friend. Meanwhile, go through your own answers to each of these questions ahead of time; that way, you'll be able to respond easily to the questions your new friend will probably ask you, and you'll create a real conversation that flows comfortably. This **M.A.P. Y.O.U.** formula makes networking easy because it helps you get to know your new friend and to focus your conversation to ensure you're spending your time wisely.

So now that you're all ready and have a clear mind, let's go in! Look at the following diagram. Note that networking starts before you even walk in the door. Why? Because out in the lobby (hopefully) there is a line waiting to get in. This is your first opportunity to network. In fact, you'll even find opportunities in the parking lot, as you walk in with other people at the same time. Too often people keep their heads down and bulldoze their way in, but don't be one of them. Be the person with the bright face, chin up and ready to open the doors right away.

Before you arrive, have an icebreaker or two ready to use. I know it's an old term, but it says it all. I usually like to start with something funny or a little off base to catch their attention, such as, "I think they're taking fingerprints at the registration table." This makes the other person laugh, or stop and think and then laugh, which easily opens the door to conversation. Arrive five to ten minutes early — not too early and not too late. Do your best to arrive when you think there will be a line, and follow the diagram in this section. So while you're in line, turn around to the person behind you and use your icebreaker, "Boy I sure could use a drink." You'll obtain a chuckle from them. Now you've got an opening!

Extend your hand and introduce yourself, your name and your company name. They will return the favor. Ball goes back into your court. This is the beauty with conversations. You talk, you throw the ball, they talk, and they throw the ball back to you. You can ask them what they do, which gives you an opportunity to find out a little bit more about them before you give your capabilities statement; maybe you can tweak it to align with your new friend's business. Once you know what they do and you've responded with what you do, think of some high gain questions you already have mapped out and what you could ask next. I use what I call a "Grand Tour" question: "Tell me how you got into that business?" This allows them to loosen up and talk about themselves — and let's face it, most of us enjoy talking about ourselves. Continue with your high gain questions, but remember to keep the conversation relatively short unless you know you have found a winner.

Next, tap the shoulder of the person in front of you and introduce yourself — name and company name only — and introduce your new friend behind you to the person in front of you. You have now done something nice for your new friend; he or she will realize that you're on their side and are looking out for them. You'll use this gracious move throughout the event.

So now you have walked in the door with two new friends. See if they would like to follow you to the cocktail table. Perform the same exercise. Hopefully there is a long line at the drink table and you can turn around and introduce your two new friends to a new person behind you. Do the same with the person in front of you. You have now created your own group of friends. Take them with you to the food table. If they don't follow you, then join a new group or find the wall flower that could use some help getting off the wall or away from the food. The more you practice your process the easier it becomes, until soon you're the master networker that others look for because they know you'll help them find a new contact.

Reject the rejecter

How do you talk to someone who is aloof? You don't. Reject the rejecter. If you're not comfortable with the person you're talking to, move on! I don't care if they are the President of the United States — don't waste your time on someone who is treating you as if you're not there. Your job isn't to convince anyone. Your job is to find those who are interested in you and who interest you.

How do you handle someone who is always looking around for someone else to talk to? You don't. Once again — reject the rejecter. If they can't spend two minutes of their time on what you have to say, then excuse yourself politely and move on. You don't have time for them either.

How do you handle a group that won't let you in? Listen for a little while; if you see they are trying to keep their group closed — let them, and move on to another group.

Very few people are openly rude or hostile, but when they are, you don't need to subject yourself to this. NEVER take it personally — they obviously have their own problems and you're not the one to figure it out for them.

MORE GENERAL NETWORKING GUIDELINES

- Don't wait for people to find you — no one will come!

- Get out there and meet people.

- Don't force yourself on others. Use a great ice breaker — a little humor works wonders.

- Reach out and extend yourself.

- Move from guest behavior to host behavior; introduce your new friend to another person.

- Every person you meet has a story.

- Every person you meet has something special to share with you.

- You have many gifts, and you can share them with every person you meet.

- Every time you go out is an opportunity to give to someone.

FOLLOW-UP

Send a hand-written card of appreciation to anyone you've met with whom you think you might be able to do business. Take all the business cards you receive and run them through your card scanner or enter them manually into your database. Now you can add these new contacts to your marketing campaigns (always give them an option to opt out of the mailing list) and continue to develop and nurture your new relationships. (If you don't have a database to store your contacts, you're stuck in the 1900's. Get out now and fix this issue before you do anything else!)

Once you've gone through your cards and decided who would be good prospects, make sure that you follow through on a consistent basis. You may have to reach out to a contact many, many times before they ultimately buy from you, so stay in touch! This is where many people fall short. Then they look at that particular networking group and say it didn't work for them. Nonsense! They just didn't put enough effort into the follow-up. When you sign up for a networking group, you get what you put into it. The best way to keep involved is to become a board member or the head of a committee as soon as possible. You must become visible quickly, so as many people as possible know who you are and what you can do for them.

Consider volunteering for your favorite charity, especially if you also know there is an audience for your product. There is nothing wrong with providing your expertise to those in need. In fact, most business owners who volunteer are doing so with a marketing twist in mind. What it will do for you is provide exposure and show that you're giving back. It will also help you feel better about the time you're spending volunteering, because you know you're growing your business as well. That's the way it's done. I have recently found a charity I really enjoy — the YWCA. I can help people who are starting new companies, and at the same time, the YWCA provides fantastic fundraiser events that draw many like-minded businesses for me to speak to.

Get Those Sales!

At this point, you have an understanding of your target market and which clients will bring in the most money the soonest. You've eliminated any doubts in your mind that you'll succeed, and you feel confident talking with new people. You are ready to go out there and show the world what you have. Now you just need to get some sales!

They say there is no such thing as a born salesperson. Mainly, it just takes practice. In Chapter 2, where we talked about habits, we learned that the more times you repeat an action, the better you become — and the same holds true for sales. I can tell you that there is a set of tools you can use in sales to get through the door and close deals quickly. **Those tools are all about the client.** Simply put, as long as you're constantly thinking about what the client needs, you can't lose. The minute you think about what you can gain, you lose.

KNOWLEDGE IS POWER

Know your client

Do you remember when we talked about targeting your market? Use that knowledge now. Back up that general understanding you have of your target market with specific research on the person or company you're selling to. Especially if you're selling to other businesses, visit their website and note what you see. Is their website outdated, which might signify that they are busy and overworked and unable to keep on top of their website, or maybe that they are facing budget troubles and can't afford to update their website? Have they won any awards recently that might signify that they are serious about remaining competitive? Read up on their industry, too. Are there any particular economic or regulatory challenges the entire industry is struggling with?

Know as much as you possibly can about your client, so that you can identify their key challenges and provide solutions.

EXERCISE 3.4

List three clients you want to have:

1) _____

2) _____

3) _____

Research them, and list three things you learn about each of them:

1) _____

2) _____

3) _____

List three additional clients you want to have:

1) _____

2) _____

3) _____

Research them, and list three things you learn about each of them:

1) _____

2) _____

3) _____

Know your competition

You should also know your biggest competitor's strengths and weaknesses. Find out everything you can about what your competitor does. Why do people buy from them? Do they do things differently than you? Find out what those differences might be. Never cut down a competitor in front of a client, but instead, use what you know about the competitor to put your solutions in the most attractive light.

The first place I go to research my competition is the internet. I visit their website and analyze everything about them — from their board of directors to old and new press releases. Is there any information I can use there? You'd be surprised at how often you can turn a deal in your favor because you took the time to go deeper than the skin. Knowledge is power.

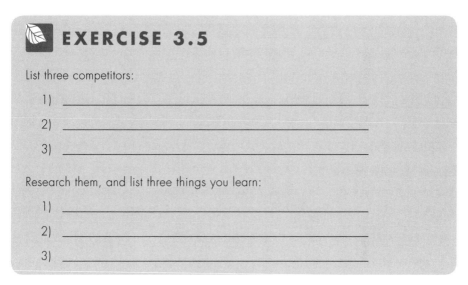

EXERCISE 3.5

List three competitors:

1) _____

2) _____

3) _____

Research them, and list three things you learn:

1) _____

2) _____

3) _____

Know your value proposition

Before you begin selling, make sure you know what makes you unique. Why should anyone buy from you? This is the time to bring out that value proposition you created in the beginning of this chapter! Also look at what makes your product unique. You might say that there isn't anything unique about your product, but I beg you to dig deeper. You obviously chose to sell or produce the particular product you have for a reason. What sold you on the idea? Why do you believe it will benefit others? You could be selling something as mundane as toilet paper. Now you might say, "Yeah, but everybody uses toilet paper." But does everyone use the same type? The answer is no. The toilet paper market is so varied that most stores devote a whole wall to display all the different kinds of toilet paper out there — amazing, isn't it? And do you think these toilet paper manufacturers have learned everything about their clients and how they use (no pun intended!) their products and adjusted their marketing accordingly? Of course they have! Remember when colored toilet paper was all the rage? The point is — targeting your ideal client is crucial.

 EXERCISE 3.6

Always remember: when you share you get back. What do you want people to hear from you?

- What is your value proposition to yourself and others?

- How are you and your business different from others?

- What can you offer, in your own unique way, that no one else on this planet can give?

- Why should the client listen to you?

- How can you help the client?

Know your product

The great thing about being an entrepreneur is that you can customize everything about your product or services to fit any client's needs. You control your company. If you really want to get into a client, use them as a Beta test site. Let them test drive the product for free for a couple of months, especially if you see a large future ahead with this client.

I did this recently with a new product I was introducing to the market. One of my competitors was offering a product with some similar features for a fraction of the price of my product. The first thing I did was to create a product comparison which showed the differences between my product and the competitor's product. This became an immediate sales tool that I could use with new clients. I then identified a potential client I felt would be a good match, and I found out how much revenue this company earned every time they made a sale. I went on to explain to the client that if my product helped them make even one additional sale, it would pay for itself.

If you can guarantee to your client that your product or service will help them increase revenue, you will close more sales. As your client uses your services, they will establish a strong connection with your services and won't want to use anything else.

EXERCISE 3.7

List three aspects of your product and compare them to the competition. If you do not yet have the business built or a product developed, realize the "ideas" are still there. This will help in your development of these ideas.

Your Product	**Your Competition's Product**
1) _____	1) _____
2) _____	2) _____
3) _____	3) _____

Know how to treat your client

Everyone wants to be treated special, so show your prospects that you care. Call them by their first names. Offer a firm handshake. Pay attention to what you see in their office or facility. And above all, let them know that you are there to help them.

Let's assume you've done your homework on both your prospective new client and your competition. You can now use this information to get to the next level. When you contact your new client, you can lead with what you already know about their company and your competition. **Explain to your client that you have** **a solution for them that they might not have thought about.** Bring up one of those unique areas about you and your company that you know provides that over-the-top quality, and don't let it go. Don't sell, either; the point is to provide information for solutions that solve their problems. If they don't remember their prior conversation with you, well, make this one memorable. Don't bother asking if they got your brochure, and don't belittle yourself by saying that you're "just checking in." YOU ARE THERE BECAUSE YOU CAN HELP THEM — SO LET THEM KNOW THAT!

I've already shown you that your prospect doesn't care about you or what you're selling. They just want to know that you'll deliver results. This requires you to take action. And more than that, you have to *finish* the action. Be the consultant and problem solver that you are, and keep true to your promises.

Are you familiar with Maslow's hierarchy of needs? Essentially Maslow says that people need to take care of their most basic needs before they can focus on anything else. This psychological theory certainly seems to hold true in the business world as well.

Your job as an entrepreneur and a salesperson is to take care of your client's basic needs first. It's important for you to make your clients feel safe and secure, so they trust you and your product or service. Once you have built trust, you can continue to build your relationship with your client on a strong foundation. Show them that you care, show them results from the very beginning, and continue to show this throughout every aspect of your dealings with them.

 Know your product, and keep a list of how your product or future product can benefit your client or future client. No limit on this one — list, list, list and list…

Know what to expect

Make sure your dreams are measurable. And do me a favor; stop calling them dreams! Instead, promise me you will live these dreams here and now. You are the force in your life. Don't play small.

Dreams will remain dreams if you don't put them into action today. Expand. Expect the absolute ultimate, every day of your life. Starting now.

EXERCISE 3.8

Come up with any comments, both positive and negative, that may arise when you present your product or service to your client. Know what to expect from the client before you walk in the door. Be prepared; list three benefits and three objections and how you will handle the objections.

	Benefits	Objections	How you will handle the objections
1)			
2)			
3)			

Know when to stop

IS IT DEAD YET???

It's important to make follow-up calls if you don't get a sale the first time you speak with a new company. And remember, your follow-up calls can provide a unique experience for the prospect — so don't call and say you're "just checking in!" Don't waste your time or theirs; make that call a meaningful experience that they will remember and that will move them into action more quickly. Send them a card, a gift certificate, flowers, anything! I guarantee to you, very few competitors will go to this length.

However, if you find yourself faced with someone who just refuses to buy from you, sometimes you just have to give it up. It's not worth it to keep chasing a dead lead, I don't care who it is! Try to get through to the company six times, and that is more than enough. Any more than that and you become a stalker. As my mother always told me, "Go find bigger fish in the sea."

WHERE TO START?

Identify and work your circle of influencers

Well, I guess THIS is where the rubber meets the road! If you don't have clients, you don't have a business — right? We've just walked you through some of the mechanics of preparing for the sale. But where do you start? Who should you reach out to first?

You'll find my secret to obtaining clients will be one of the easiest things you've ever done. So many times we just don't see what is right in front of us. We go out searching the world for someone who will listen, when our audience is literally standing there staring at us. What do I mean? Finding clients is simple; you just have to understand two key points:

1. You have a unique circle of personal connections — I call this your "circle of influencers."

2. Every individual in your circle of influencers has their own circle of influencers, and so on and so on.

So let's figure out how to leverage your circle of influencers to build your client base now!

EXERCISE 3.9

Write down the names of every person in your life who has an influence on what you do and how you do it. Next, write down their relationship to you. How much time do you spend with these people? Are they negative people or positive people? Do they support you in your business or not? Circle the individual who has the most positive influence in your life.

Influencer's Name	Relationship	Time Spent	Negative or Positive	Do They Support Your Business

Can you turn the negative influencers into positive influencers? If you can't, then limit your time with them — or throw them out the door! Don't poison yourself with negative thoughts from anyone.

If you could add someone to your list, who would it be? Dream big. Identify an influencer who is big in your industry, someone you really want to meet, and someone who will give you such a guiding light your business will explode. Next, write down two ways you'll reach out to that individual to begin the process of meeting them. When will you take these two steps? Pick a date and time and write it down.

Each of these people has their own list of influencers as well. See if you can identify, for each person in your list, three people from their list. Do you see any cross over in names? Would you like to add any of those names to your own list? Can you ask your influencers for introductions?

Focus first on the individuals you know. Work with your first level of influencers and build upon that. Ask for introductions, based upon whom you know and whom they know. This is one of the most natural ways to grow your business. Your influencers are the people you trust and with whom you can share information. By actively expanding your circle, you'll see your business grow as well.

EXERCISE 3.9 *continued*

If your influencers don't know your business, then sit down with them, one on one, and explain to them what your new company does. Remember your value proposition? Explain it to them! Develop a list of questions to ask your influencers when you meet. Who do your influencers know whom you should also be talking to? Have a goal of getting one introduction from each person in your circle of influencers. This goal will provide nourishment to the conversation and help your influencers open up new channels for you to grow your business.

I guarantee this works! We are all connected, and you're especially connected to your influencers, and they are to their own influencers, and so on — until we are all virtually interconnected with everyone on this planet.

Scour your Facebook friends, LinkedIn connections and Twitter followers — and everyone you are following as well. Identify people with whom you can connect from your own list and social media lists.

Of course, this whole exercise may take you out of your comfort zone a little. But to become an entrepreneur, you must embrace the change and make it happen. If you don't, no one — and I mean no one — will do it for you. You've got to act again and again to create a strong and powerful network of influencers. The more powerful your network, the more powerful you'll become…all because of the people with whom you're associating. Plain and simple, you create your own destiny and your own circle of influence.

Opportunity comes in many packages. The most important thing for you to do as an entrepreneur is to put it out there. Have people recognize that you're looking for opportunity. Take action to bring opportunity into your life.

As you talk with each of your influencers, understand that something about you has drawn each of them to you. Therefore, they all have YOU in common. As you have your discussions with each of them, make it about more than just you; try to help them, as well. Think about how you can connect each of your influencers together, which in turn will build a stronger network of influencers. The more you give — the more you provide opportunities for your influencers — the more they will repay you with clients or with whatever other resources they can offer. Give and receive — it's that simple. Always look for ways to connect your influencers and provide back to them. You'll grow ten-fold in return.

As I have said before, take off the blinders and simply open your eyes to the reality that you are the catalyst to your future. You have already begun building your fortress with strong connections that overlap connections that overlap connections. If you take all of the business cards you have acquired over the years, you would be surprised by the sheer number of people you have met. The first time I did this, I had over 3,000 contacts! Contacts are power…but only if you stay in touch. So go ahead and reach out to people you haven't talked to in a while. Even if you haven't talked to someone in ten years, you might be surprised that they are still relevant to your life, and that you might still be able to help each other.

If you keep doing what you've always done, you'll never get any better results. Branch out. Take action. Try something new. You can do it!

FINE-TUNE YOUR APPROACH TO SALES

I use a very simple code — A.C.T. — to help me sell more:

Axis: Center on the Customer

Communication: Build Trust Quickly

Trigger: Solicit desired responses from the Client

Axis: Center on the customer

Customers are number one. Always. They are the axis to your business. As you build your relationship with your customers, you'll become a valued part of their business. I typically will lead into a client relationship with one product. As you continue to converse with your client and center your focus on their needs, you will find that you have other products or services that will help them as well. Don't be afraid of expanding that conversation. Remember you are the expert and you have the tools to keep that client happy and take their business to the next level. Show them how.

Communication: Build trust quickly

Communication is the key to building trust. It also helps to understand right from the beginning the type of personality you're dealing with. Many times we go into a meeting focused on our own personality — our own way of thinking — without even paying attention to the person across the table. This isn't the way to make friends and influence people. There are four categories of personalities — those who are bullet point people (usually the CEO), those who are analytics (usually the CFO), those who are personality people (usually the sales people), and those who are always there to help with the details (usually administrative).

We'll talk about these categories of personality more in the next section, but for now, know that if you go into a meeting without recognizing the type of person with whom you'll be talking, you can lose the sale from the beginning. Why? Because from the moment you walk in the door you won't be listening properly. What is the first code of selling? The axis — to center on the customer. That means understanding who you're going to talk to before you walk in the door, and adjusting your approach accordingly in order to speak their language and build their trust.

I've said this before, but it's critical that you do your research and understand everything you can about your prospect. If circumstances absolutely prevented you from doing your research on this particular client, then at a bare minimum, pay attention to the person's job title. Take a few moments to observe the client before you begin talking. Note what their office looks like. Do they have a lot of awards (potentially a personality person), are there certifications/credentials (probably an analytic), are there lots of family or pet pictures (probably helpful person), or are there fewer personal and more company oriented wall hangings (probably bullet point)?

Of course these are assumptions, but if you're not familiar with the person, at least it's a start. From here, you can begin to understand the type of individual with whom you're working.

Trigger: Solicit desired responses from the client

In order to obtain the responses you want, you will need to understand what the client wants and needs — which could be two distinctly different things. The only way to do this is to actively listen, by asking high gain questions which will bring out those areas that are most important to the client. Many times a client will *need* specific basic services to start, but over the long run they may *want* more of the added benefits and bells and whistles that make their job easier and allow them to create an over-the-top product. Look for the triggers through your line of questioning, and be prepared to make a difference by triggering responses beyond the "need" status.

Let's take a look at different types of personalities and analyze the approach you should take with each personality to trigger the responses you want.

UNDERSTAND TYPICAL CUSTOMER PERSONALITIES

The Driver: The business owner or director

This person is like the lighthouse, guiding their company through the rocky shores of the business world. The Driver wants to know how your solution fits into the big picture of the company. They'll make their decision based on bullet points of information, so don't bother them with the details. Usually they'll have someone else analyze the fine points of your product anyway. When you're working with the Driver, give them your concept, your value proposition, and why your product or service will alleviate their pain. If you can show the Driver why you can solve their problem, then you'll have a sale. But that means observing their personality type.

If you walk in that door with the wrong approach — say you're all chatty or making too much small talk about things that have nothing to do with their business or him or her personally, then you might as well stay home. Do your homework before you walk in the door. If you don't feel that you know what the Driver is looking for, then be prepared to ask high gain questions that will make the difference in your ability to close the deal. These high gain questions will give you the credibility you need to make the sale. We've talked about these questions briefly already, and in the next section we'll go into more detail.

The Analytic: CFOs, accountants, engineers, technology people

The description alone pretty much explains this person. The Analytic wants all the details. Again, when you walk in the door, no messing around. Of course in all situations you want to develop rapport, but not too much small talk. The Analytic wants to know why you're there. Can you increase their bottom line? Can you decrease their cost? Do you offer a higher quality product than what they already use? Their job is to analyze all the options, so be prepared and have ALL your facts ready.

Your high gain questions may well be the same with any of the personalities, but the difference will be in how you approach each conversation. Like the Driver, the Analytic isn't one for small talk. You'll gain immediate credibility by providing a lot of facts, figures and information that isn't fluff.

Expressive: Sales

This person is looking for attention. They're usually not afraid to express their feelings. They make friends easily and are always willing to hear what you have to offer, but frankly, they're going to be more interested in themselves and what they have to say. They are not as detail-oriented as the Driver or the Analytic, and they will have a tendency to sell OR buy. They might not follow through. However, a great salesperson has learned how to tame many of these issues and uses their unique ability to connect and build relationships with the other personalities to close deals and maintain long-term clients.

To sell to this person, use your high gain questions to get to the bottom of any issues they may have. You want to make sure you understand what issues they may be facing and how you can provide your services to them. They can have Driver tendencies as well, so the best way to sell to them is to obtain the bottom-line facts through questioning, so that you can provide a solution.

Amiable: Administrative people

These people care about everyone around them. They want to please, and they want to provide as much information as possible in the right way to those who depend on him or her. They avoid conflict and want to have everything go smoothly for everyone.

When you're selling to this individual, your use of high gain questions will be very important. This person will have a tendency to agree with you in person to avoid conflict, even though they won't buy from you in the end. This is why you'll need to follow a line of questioning that ensures you're getting to the bottom of what they need so that you can elicit the desired response from them.

MAKE THE SALES CALL

You'll note that I typically refer to prospects as clients. I like to think of every prospect as a client, therefore, why would I refer to them as a prospect? If you can see the end result in your mind, and use language that depicts the end you foresee, you'll make that image become your reality.

There is really no mystery to selling. In fact, think about how you like to be sold. You want someone to give you their undivided attention, you want them to relate to you as a person and to build rapport, and you want them to provide to you completely accurate information based upon what you need. It's as simple as that.

People like to say that they hate selling. But the truth is that everyone is a salesperson, whether they want to admit it or not. The minute you start to interact with someone else, you're selling something. It may be your personality, a particular view point, or a solution to a problem. When you're with a customer, you want to do just that.

So here's how you do it.

First, don't forget the breath mint

I would prefer not to have to mention this, but it's ABSOLUTELY imperative that if you're going to meet people, you must have impeccable hygiene — from your hair to your shoes. Make sure your teeth are in good order as well; if they are stained, get them cleaned. Always use a breath mint, mouthwash or spray (not gum) before going into a meeting. Nothing is more disgusting than bad breath and dirty teeth, hair or body during a meeting — you lose! Make sure you dress well. If possible, dress a step higher than you normally would. Casual wear isn't acceptable — I don't care what kind of business your client is in. You don't dress down unless they ask you to, and that won't happen until they feel you're part of the family.

Okay, glad that's out of the way. Sorry, but it just had to be said!

Opening the conversation

Here's where the fun begins — with something called the "**M.A.P.**" process that we briefly introduced in the networking section of this chapter. You will notice that **M.A.P**. stands for the same words, but the definitions have changed based upon the next level in the sales process. In the opening of a sale, you want to address three key areas to ensure you and your client are both on the same page:

Motive: Why are you there?

Advantage: How will you help your customer?

Probe: Make sure this is the direction your customer wants to go.

Motive

Begin by M.A.P.ping the direction of the sell. Make sure that you both know why you're there and that you both understand the conclusion that you're looking for. This lets you find out in the very beginning whether or not you're sitting in front of a potential buyer. Of course you should qualify your appointments before you meet face-to-face, but sometimes we miss the mark. That is why the opening of the sale is critical to the continued discussion.

Capabilities Statement

Do you remember this from our discussion on networking? Just as you used your capabilities statement when starting conversations at networking events, you'll also use your capabilities statement in any type of sales call. Even if you've already told your capabilities statement to the client when you set the appointment, bringing it up at the beginning of the meeting will set the stage for the rest of the meeting. Tailor your statement to what you've learned from your research and from any prior conversations with the client. This will be a great starting place for your ongoing conversation with your client.

Your capabilities statement should take no more than 30 seconds. Many times (DINI) people make their capabilities statements so long or complicated that no one can understand what they are selling. Here's another simple code — **Y.O.U.** — to help you stick with three main points:

You: Your name and company name, plus title to lend credibility

Own: What your company does, your product or service, and your clients

Unique: The benefit you give your clients

Here's how the Y.O.U. code works in action:

You: Hi, I'm Holly Katko, the President of U-Connect!

Own: We help entrepreneurs start their companies by eliminating the barriers they have set before themselves.

Unique: What makes us unique is that we nail what's stopping our clients from moving forward and then we proceed to guide them in the development of a successful business.

This capability statement is a little vague, but it's vague on purpose. You want your statement to provide enough information for the client to get a sense of who you are, but vague enough to prompt the client to ask questions, therefore giving you more floor time to provide a little more information and throw the ball back into their court so you can qualify them.

For example, the client might ask, "That's interesting. How do you do that?" Your answer would be to explain the next level of detail of your product. In this case I would say, "We create customized programs to address those areas that stop people from getting to the next level in their lives, whether it's erasing bad habits, learning how to sell, opening the doors to a new business, or eliminating fear in their lives. We have more than fifteen different programs that can be delivered online and in person."

Now hopefully this level of the conversation would have taken place prior to the face-to-face meeting, but it's still a good refresher to begin the meeting. Also, you'll want to refer to your prior conversation with your client so you can now open the door to understanding their needs.

Advantage

To work this step of the **M.A.P.** code, you'll need to have some tools in your pocket: namely, an understanding of how you want the rest of the sell to go. Keep in mind you're always in control of the call. You want to make sure that you get what you came for. The natural progression of the call begins with connecting with the client, which you have done at this point, and then encouraging the client to provide the information you need to fill their needs. This will set the stage for you to understand the advantages your product can give to the client.

In order for you to recognize your client's needs, you'll begin probing for the answers to critical questions…which leads naturally to the next step of the code.

Probe

To keep the sales call moving forward, you'll need to develop a line of questioning. But this isn't just any type of questioning. This is asking questions that you could not find the answers to on a piece of paper — questions that will help build your relationship and your proposal.

At this point, you may feel like you're ready to jump into closing the sale and to begin providing your services or product to your client…but no matter how tempting this may be, you're not really ready yet! Realize that you still know relatively little about the client, and you need to understand them fully before you can begin to help them. Remember that the point is not to sell to them. You're there to *help* them.

There are different lines of probing questions you can ask. You might ask simple questions that need only a yes or no response. You might ask questions gleaned from information you found on the client's website. Or you might choose to ask questions that elicit intelligent, thought provoking answers. We will concentrate on the last group. Now don't get me wrong, I'm not telling you to sit in this meeting and hound the poor client. There's nothing I hate more than someone who interrogates me like a private investigator trying to get a murder confession out of me. This will put anyone on the defensive! Instead, I'm talking about developing questions that you can easily ask during the conversation and that allow you to understand the client more clearly.

I have developed over 100 questions for each of my product lines. Does that mean I use all of them during a call? What do you think? Of course not! But when you're in front of someone and you get nervous, having these questions readily available is what will make the difference between you and the competition. The categories and the questions you'll develop will follow the natural flow of a conversation. Read on to learn more.

ASK "HIGH GAIN" QUESTIONS

When you're probing, be prepared with at least five areas where you'd like to have additional information about the client and their company. Use those areas to develop qualifying questions that will clarify the client's needs and how you can help, so that you can increase your ability to close the deal.

I've developed the following chart to help you understand the ebb and flow of these high gain questions:

Start the sales call by focusing on the person sitting in front of you, not the company – at least for now. People like to talk about themselves, so this opens the person up and gets the conversation comfortably started. Ask the client what they do, how they got into this business and what they did before this.

Once you've both opened up a little and you feel like you know the person a little better, you can start asking questions about the company. You don't want to ask surface questions with easy answers, but deeper questions that get the client to think. Use leading words like "who," "what", "when," "where," "why," and "how" to entice the client to go deeper with their explanation. For instance, you might ask, "What changes have you seen in your business, your competition, or your products in the last three years?" "Why do you feel these changes have happened?" "How do you feel these changes will affect your business in the coming year?"

Ask your client what they're doing now about their problems, and what else they've been considering. Many times the reason you're being brought in is because they want something new — the latest and greatest — so slow down and find out what they've been thinking about. Explore new ideas. This is actually a great hidden opportunity for you; sure, you can obtain a new client, but this is also the perfect time and place to start thinking about how to build a new mouse trap based upon what your client tells you!

By asking these thought-provoking questions, you'll be amazed how quickly you and your client will get wrapped up in the conversation. Both of you will be focused on creating that perfect product and fulfilling that need that takes the client where they want to be.

Remember to direct the questioning based upon answers you will need for developing your proposal. Random questioning will get you nowhere. Specific questioning shows that you know your product and that you care. What are the client's wants and needs? Here is a short list of questions to get you started developing your own high gain questions. Fill in additional questions based upon how you want to steer the conversation toward your product or service.

 EXERCISE 3.10

COMPANY AND CONTACT

1. When did the business start?

2. How long have you been with the company?

3. What did you start out doing for the company?

4. What divisions are in the company?

5. Who owns the company?

EXERCISE 3.10 *continued*

6. Do you make all the buying decisions for the company?

7. Who else does?

8. _____

9. _____

10. _____

NEEDS AND WANTS

1. What do you need from a vendor?

2. What else?

3. What matters most to you: price, quality or service?

4. What do you not want?

5. If there was one thing that you could ask for in a company, what would it be?

6. _____

7. _____

8. _____

9. _____

10. _____

COMPANY-SPECIFIC

1. How many _____ do you have?

2. How are they used?

3. Do you have other products/services as well?

4. Are there other locations?

5. _____

6. _____

7. _____

EXERCISE 3.10 *continued*

8. _____
9. _____
10. _____

COMPETITION

1. Who do you currently use?

2. What do you like about them?   Price   Quality   Service

3. What don't you like about them?   Price   Quality   Service

4. If there was one thing you could ask from a vendor, what would it be?

5. _____
6. _____
7. _____
8. _____
9. _____
10. _____

BUDGET

1. What is typically the budget?

2. Who is in charge of the budget?

3. How much or what percentage of the budget is for _____?

4. _____
5. _____
6. _____
7. _____
8. _____
9. _____
10. _____

EXERCISE 3.10 *continued*

NEXT STEPS

1. Do you need another meeting? If so, when?

2. Do you need to do a proposal? If so, set the next meeting date now.

3. Do you need to set up a site visit? If so do it now.

4. Do you need to interview other people in the company? If so set it up now.

5. Do you need to meet someone else in the company? If so do it or set it up now.

6. Sign the contract now.

7. _____

8. _____

9. _____

10. _____

WHAT HAPPENS NEXT?

So at this point, you've built rapport and advanced the sale by asking the right questions. **Now is a good time to take a moment to make sure you and your client are on the same page, by confirming your understanding of where they are and what they would like to see in your product.** This is a critical point. Establishing a clear understanding of where you both are will bring you directly into closing the sale. Why? Because you have already asked everything you need to know, so there should be no surprises in the end.

The next step is to either close the deal now or to set the next appointment if you need to provide a proposal. End the meeting with a resounding "yes." Outline the next step to your client, make sure they are ready to take that step, and set a date to finalize things. Never leave a meeting without setting the next step.

Diagram of the sales process

The following is a diagram of one of my products. This is the type of diagram you'll use in selling, networking or anytime you want to know deeper information about your client. I recommend that you start at the top and develop the questions clockwise. As you get closer to the end of the circle, you'll complete the sales cycle. You'll note there are many questions that I can pull from to obtain the valid information I need to close the deal.

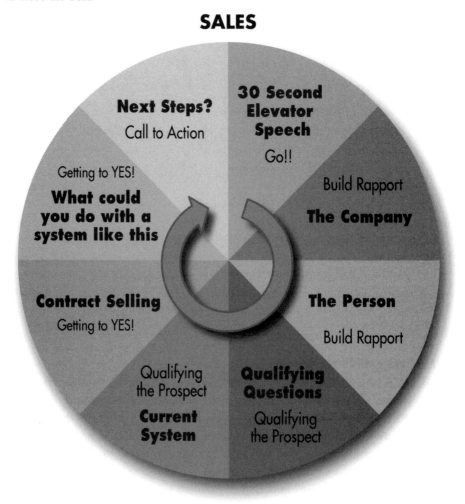

EXERCISE 3.11

Go ahead and list who you think could be your first ten clients right now. Put them in order — who will buy 1st, 2nd and so on.

What services/products will you sell to each of them? At what price?

What will be the total income from all ten of these new clients? Monthly? Annually?

What will be the next service/product you will sell to them? When?

CHAPTER 4

KEEP MOVING FORWARD

Create Long-Term Clients

THE OTHER DAY, ONE OF MY CLIENTS CALLED ME; as we were wrapping the conversation up, he casually mentioned, "Holly, by the way, I'm playing golf with one of your other clients. We'll be trading notes on you!" Well, I knew this was no joke! Who would have thought that two of my clients in two different towns in two completely different businesses would be playing golf together in the same foursome! Ohhhh my gosh! Luckily both of these clients were strong, long-term relationships I had built over time. (Although really, there was no "luck" to it!)

I cannot stress enough how important it is to establish long-term clients. I'm not one to go out and play a round of golf with my clients (a little more practice and I will be!), but I'm one to keep up on my industry and make sure that I know whatever product or service I'm offering like the back of my own hand. I make sure to know as much as possible about my products, my client and my industry, so that when (not if) the competition comes knocking at my client's door, I have a better mouse trap.

Okay. Of course, no one knows what will happen in the future and whether a client will stay with you over the long haul. So you have a choice to make; you can sit and worry about what might happen (which really is the root of all evil!), or you can take action to ensure most — if not all — of your clients will stay with you for years.

LOOK FOR WAYS TO ADD VALUE

When performing work for any client, **always give 110%**. Provide more than they are paying for. Go above and beyond their expectations. I do this for some of my consulting clients. For free, I may research and provide additional information to help educate my clients on particular areas, or I may accompany my clients to meetings or to networking events to help build their confidence. Establish up front where you can provide additional value, so you can easily build this value into the project. And make sure your extra effort doesn't go unnoticed; maybe you add it on the final invoice, with the words "FREE" or "NO CHARGE" instead of a dollar cost. Or you can provide a dollar value for the services, and then zero them out with a discount right below it. This establishes with the client that you went above and beyond expectations, but it also reminds them that usually those free services do have value. It is also gives you a good time to ask for referrals.

EXPAND WITHIN YOUR EXISTING CLIENTS

It's important to continually look for ways to expand your business with your existing clients, to allow you to build a solid foundation for your business. Even if your product or service is typically a one-time project-based purchase, begin thinking about building long-term relationships. If you have really proven yourself on that first project with a client, then you should propose working on new projects or in another division of the company. As you continue to work with your clients, you'll notice other areas into which you can expand.

ASK FOR REFERRALS

When asking for a referral, **ask the client** if they will call the referral first so it becomes a personal referral. In fact, it's even better if your client is willing to conference you in on a call so you can talk directly to the new client! When you obtain a referral, always send your current client a gift card or some token of appreciation that you know he or she would enjoy.

DELIVER OUTSTANDING CUSTOMER SERVICE

When it all comes right down to it, the only thing that really matters is the client. If we don't treat the client right, we don't have a business. In this day and age (which really isn't any different from the past), if we provide over-the-top customer service, we are rewarded with more money, more referrals, and the satisfaction of knowing we did the best we could and more!

Treat your clients with loving care. We all know the amount of time and effort it takes to replace a client…and that doesn't even count the damage a single irate client can cause when they broadcast to the world their dissatisfaction with your company.

The six rules you see in this section are nothing new. We all know these rules, and know we need to apply them to our business model, day in and day out. We need to build a plan of action based upon these rules so they are never broken. Make sure that all your employees follow these rules. Build these rules into their performance reviews. Follow through and measure the usage of these rules and reward those employees that use them on a consistent basis.

Let's look at each one individually.

Customer Service Rule #1: Respect your client's time

NEVER LEAVE THE CUSTOMER WAITING. Try a little experiment: In the middle of a busy work day, don't do or say anything for 30 seconds. How does it feel? Uncomfortable? Irritating? Like that 30 seconds just cost you $50 of your time? Probably. Guess how your customer will feel when they've had to wait because of you? So don't do it!

ARRIVE EARLY. Arrive for appointments 15 minutes early, because it's always better to be early than late. If you're going to be late, even by a minute, call. There is absolutely no reason not to call if you're going to be late. That one phone call lends so much credibility. Don't assume it's not a big deal to be 5 minutes late, because it is. Your client's time is very important, so respect it.

A NON-RESPONSE IS NO RESPONSE. If a client is waiting for an answer on some-thing, make sure you connect with the client every day until you get the answer. If you promised them you would have an answer in 2 hours, stick to it. If you can't give them an answer in two hours, let them know and tell them why. Don't leave the customer waiting. Set a company standard on how soon you'll get back to a client. Put this standard in writing and make it part of the proposal package you give to your client. This will be one of your unique features. Set the standard and stick to it.

Customer Service Rule #2: Be careful when answering questions

SEEK HELP. If you don't know the answer, DON'T make one up. Get the right answer. No short cuts here; get as much information as you can to fulfill their needs. This will help you to build your business in the future.

SEEK FIRST TO UNDERSTAND, THEN TO BE UNDERSTOOD. Steven Covey's famous line — yes! This is frequently used throughout the customer service industry and is something you should use when building your business. Listen very carefully to the client. Make sure you understand what they want.

DON'T GUESS. If you guess at the answer and guess incorrectly and then you have to sheepishly come back later with the correct answer, or if you try to hide that you didn't know the answer in the first place, people will see right through you. I don't care how good you are at bluffing; when you're talking with a client, you're trying to develop trust and respect. Neither of these comes out of a guess.

DON'T GET SLOPPY. If your paperwork is out of order, or worse, if you don't fulfill every one of the promises you have made, you'll be on the short end of the stick and so will your customer.

Customer Service Rule #3: Set high standards

FINISH WHAT YOU START. This has got to be one of the most difficult areas for people. We get all excited about a new project — we put our heads into it, we put our hearts into it. We start working it. Then a problem occurs. That's okay, we will shake it off and keep the momentum and still be excited. Then another problem occurs. Pretty soon we've grown tired of our brand new shiny toy; it has dirt all over it, and we couldn't be bothered to clean it off. The next thing you know, the project starts to fall apart. Maybe the paperwork wasn't completed properly, or maybe the promises you made are not getting done. The project has totally lost its fizzle. Stop! It's time you took responsibility. That means cleaning up loose ends before they become loose ends. Make sure to handle each situation once. Make sure all ends are tied down and your project is ready for anyone to come in and take over where you left off.

This is an essential key to client service and to the infrastructure of your company. If one person in your company isn't doing their job completely, then the whole house of cards will fall down.

Here are two simple tips for setting high standards:

- Paperwork: Do it immediately, do it right, check it twice. You don't want to touch it again.

- Promises: If you make them, follow through. It's easy to get carried away when we make promises, but if you don't follow through with every promise you make, you will have completely lost your credibility and hard feelings will begin to surface in the relationship. Do a checklist that includes all parties in your company who need to be informed about that promise, to ensure that all parties involved within your company will help you keep that promise.

Customer Service Rule #4: Avoid putting up facades

Be honest and real. Fake people are out! I think this is pretty self-explanatory. Many times when our confidence is low, we put on a facade that we hope no one else can see through. The problem is, everyone can see through it. We build facades when we really don't know ourselves and we believe someone other than ourselves will better fit the situation. This has nothing to do with communication. This is about you being you. The more real you are, the more relaxed the client will be. Some warning signs that you may be putting on a facade are:

- You're being too animated

- You're being too harsh

- You're laughing too much

- You're talking and not listening

- You're selling or fixing a problem before you know the client's needs

If you're not in your natural state, the client will distrust you. They won't be as ready to open up with their ideas and to share how they would like to see your services help them. What they'll see is someone hiding behind a wall, not someone sincere or with their needs in mind. And they don't need a superficial answer to their problems. They'll conclude that if they work with you, the project will not get done with THEM in mind. At best they'll get a cookie cutter attempt at meeting their needs.

You must have your heart in every situation to ensure that your sincerity comes through loud and clear on the only side that matters — your client's.

Customer Service Rule #5: Nurture your relationships

STAY IN TOUCH. Touches are absolutely imperative in maintaining a long-term relationship with the client.

You should have a systematic approach in place so you can consistently stay in touch with all of your clients. You can send out regular newsletters, or you can expand on this model and add an occasional gift or survey…but whatever it is, make it consistent. This will help your client to expect it and, therefore, always have you top of mind.

Also, send out an unforgettable card during the year. I have an attorney from 16 years ago who still sends me a holiday card on Christmas; it's always a funny joke, and it's the only card I remember out of all the cards I get. It's simple and inexpensive, but memorable.

PERFORMANCE REVIEWS. Make sure to monitor the usage of your relationship nurturing system to ensure it's being used by everyone. Include this system in your employee performance reviews to ensure that your staff is using the system and that they know they will be graded on the use of it. Measurable, consistent data will allow you to track the effectiveness of your system while you measure your employees' performance.

Customer Service Rule #6: Give them a WOW!

LET THE CLIENT KNOW THEY MATTER. A WOW is that unique way of telling a client that they are important. An oldie but goodie is the story where some-one tried to return tires to a Nordstrom's store. The clerk could have argued and refused to accept the tires, since Nordstrom's is a clothing store that does not sell tires. Instead, the clerk accepted the tires and gave the customer his money back. Now that is what I call service above and beyond.

There is also the story of the cab driver who transformed his cab into something closer to a limousine. His cab was impeccable. He provided snacks, hot coffee and beverages. He also made it a point to remember you if you traveled a lot and to always be on the lookout for ways to be of service to you. These extra amenities didn't cost him much, but what it did give him was returning customers and the satisfaction of knowing he was the exception in the business.

These WOWs are what set you apart from the competition. A great way to give a personal WOW is to keep a detailed client contact list with all the usual basic infor-mation that all the other vendors would have, but also with the birth dates of your client and his or her children, their graduation dates, and so on. Build a list of per-sonal data on each of your clients, and use that data, to show you care and to stand out from the crowd.

How to listen: 7 things NOT to do

I can't state enough how important customer service is to your business. This customer-focused approach should permeate everything that everyone in your company does! Consider the difference that outstanding service makes to you when you are a customer. **Think of a recent time where you called a company** **help line but you didn't receive the help you had expected.** Think of those things that the person said on the other end of the line that almost immediately led you to lose trust in the company. Well, reverse this role and remember how you wanted to be treated, so that you can treat your client the same way. Above all, DO NOT:

1. **ALLOW INTERRUPTIONS.** Stay focused on the call. Don't let other calls or other people around you interrupt the call. It's important to stay focused.

2. **MAKE UP ANSWERS.** Don't be afraid of not having the answers on the spot. If you don't have the answer, don't make it up. Even little white lies will come back to haunt you. Always tell the client you'll get back to them — don't guess.

3. **ACT LIKE YOU KNOW MORE THAN THE CLIENT.** This will cause you to interrupt or dismiss or even resolve the call before you have completely heard the issue. Wait until you have heard the issue in its entirety before you talk. This will allow the client to get it off of their chest and will clear the path for you to provide the solution.

4. **INTERRUPT A CLIENT.** Unless the client is completely out of control (never take abuse from a client), stay focused and write down your interpretation of the problem. Don't internalize the complaint; keep it business related.

5. **OVER-REACT.** A client may hit your "hot buttons," but don't let them push you out of control. Any time you lose control, you lose. Remember, this is a business. Your reaction must be of the highest caliber of professionalism. If it's not, you lose in a big way — not only the client, but your trust and credibility. These are not easy things to get back.

6. **PSEUDO-LISTEN.** If you're not listening with all your senses, then you're not listening. Trust me, the client can tell if you're slumped in your chair or thinking about something else or typing an email to

a friend while they are on the phone. The client is very intuitive, just like you. Focus.

7. **ASSUME SOMETHING CAN'T BE DONE.** Always take the extra time to think outside the box. If an issue has come up once, it will probably come up again. So come up with a new solution, and make sure to document your solution so people who are new to your company will know how to handle the situation in the future.

 EXERCISE 4.1

Answer the following questions and begin to set your company customer service policies. These policies will become part of the company and incorporated into each employee's review process.

- What is your commitment to responding to client questions?

- When a lead comes in, how quickly will your company respond?

- How quickly will you get pricing to a client? (If you are developing a new product, do not give a price at the meeting. Go back to your office and make sure you have thought of all the costs and the profit margin you wish to make.)

- How soon will you turn around proposals?

- How quickly will you resolve problems or issues clients have? Outline the different types of problems and return call commitment you will give.

 EXERCISE 4.2

List common problems that you currently experience or anticipate you might have one day.

List three solutions.

Build this list of problems and solutions to give to all of your staff. Educate them and give them a written explanation on how to handle each one of these situations. You will find that by being prepared, you can create authority with the client and have a solution readily available.

EXERCISE 4.2 *continued*

One of the best tools you can use is a decision tree. Create "if/then" scenarios and make sure this model becomes part of your policies and procedures. Because you'll want all of your staff to handle situations in the same manner, you'll need procedures for every single type of situation — so that when any client calls, they will receive the same answer from anyone on your staff. Consistency is imperative to great customer service. Make sure your staff knows how to handle difficult situations, and make sure they know the secrets to over-the-top customer service that you will offer to every client. This will get your clients to come back for more and to offer more referrals, too.

 EXERCISE 4.3

Now, outline your complete, formal customer service policy. Make sure that all employees — from product engineers to payroll clerks – know what to expect and that they all are following the same policy.

Also, share parts of this policy with your clients. This will let clients develop realistic expectations so they know, for example, if a return phone call will come immediately or after a few days. Don't set unrealistic expectations for yourself or your client. If you consistently miss the target time, than you begin to lose credibility.

Be Prepared for Bumps in the Road

WHEN YOUR CUSTOMER IS UPSET

We usually get hit with the irate customer over the phone. Sometimes it happens in person, but usually it's a situation where the client runs into an immediate problem, they want an immediate solution, and so they call you up on the phone to make it your problem. Realize first of all that there will automatically be a disconnect in this situation; you have no idea what this client's issue is, so it will take you a few minutes to catch up. **So listen carefull**y as the customer talks (or rants and raves, as the case may be), and remember that although we speak 125 to 150 words per minute, we listen and understand more than 400 words per minute. Use your mental quickness wisely. Carefully consider the information that your client has given to you.

Sometimes, due to our mental quickness, we jump ahead and miss what the client is trying to tell us. Let the client explain the issue, but don't respond right away. Just sit quietly and take notes. Soon the client might even ask if you are still there on the line. Tell the client that you have been busy taking notes. Empathize, but don't sympathize. Ask if there is anything else they would like to say, and then repeat the issue back to the client. Taking notes and repeating them back to the client not only focuses you on what the client is saying, but it also lets you make sure you understand clearly what is troubling the client.

Resist the urge to provide the solution immediately, unless the solution is completely obvious to you. Give yourself time to contemplate the situation. Make sure you provide solutions only after you have fully understood the problem and weighed several possible courses of action.

Voice

The tone of your voice reveals quite a lot when you're in a charged situation. If you find yourself faced with an agitated client in an irrational state, keep your tone neutral. Don't fall into the same pattern as the client. Remain calm, and keep your energy high. Don't internalize the issue either; again, remain calm and alert. Follow these five voice quality ideas to keep both you and the client calm:

- **ALERTNESS**. Spark and energy! This higher level of alertness will help the client to see and hear that you care.

- **PLEASANTNESS**. Make sure your voice isn't jarring or whiney. There's nothing more irritating than a whiner, and remember, your client is irritated already. Your job is to remain professional in every circumstance.

- **CONVERSATIONAL TONE**. Stay conversational and calm. If the client is extremely agitated, it may be best to say you'll get back to him or her in an hour. This will give the client time to cool down a little.

- **DISTINCTNESS**. Use a clear voice, not a lazy voice; open your mouth and sit up straight. This is critical when conversing. If the client cannot understand you, or if you sound like you could care less, you will only fuel the fire as they try to get a response from you.

- **EXPRESSIVENESS**. Vary your tone and rate; build a verbal picture. This goes along with alertness. Good use of voice and tone will increase the confidence your client feels in your ability to resolve this issue.

Whatever you do, DON'T MAKE EXCUSES AND DON'T BLAME OTHERS!

When you get hit hard, it's tough to stand up and remain calm. Don't internalize the client's issue. Keep their issue at arm's length, so you can deal with it clearly and without emotion. You're there to analyze and find a solution to their problem.

Also, be prepared with the proper language to use in any situation. The best thing you can do prior to getting hit hard is to have a plan already in place. That means building scripts ready to use for typical problems a client might experience.

Remember, professionalism wins every time. Set the standard!

ALFFF

I use a very simple method called **A.L.F.F.F.** to help make sure both the client and I move forward from a problem. Rehearse this formula ahead of time, so that when a client problem really does occur, you'll be able to easily move forward with the relationship.

> **Apologize**
>
> **Listen**
>
> **Fix**
>
> **Follow up**
>
> **Fan!!**

WHEN YOU DON'T GET PAID

Always get a contract and never do work without receiving at least part of your payment upfront. Twice, as a business owner, I chose to do business with a client without a signed contract, and both times ended up in disaster. Let me tell you how it happened.

For the first client, the owner seemed to be constantly suing someone for something. He was always having his lawyer write threatening letters, and he frequently got into arguments with vendors, always looking for a way to get out of paying for something. I also noticed when I sat in on sales presentations with him that he would say he offered services that I knew he did not in fact offer. Eventually, he slowed down in paying me for my consulting services, from bi-weekly to monthly.

Yeah, you can see where this is going, can't you? In the end, I was lucky that I only lost $5,000 from this guy.

Unfortunately, my attorney told me it would cost me $5,000 in legal fees just to get my $5,000 back, so I decided unless a claim was for $25,000 or more, a lawsuit really wasn't worth it. More importantly, I learned to never let a client be in arrears for more than a month and never more than $5,000. This is imperative. Once you start the habit of allowing large amounts of past due receivables, the client will take advantage of you and won't pay on time — and why not? You've made it easy for them; you've set the precedent, and they will take it for all it's worth.

With the other client, I didn't learn from my first experience, and I let myself go into a business situation without a contract with the client. You'd think I'd know better, but the owner seemed so extremely honest to me and such a good person. I performed consulting services for him for about five or six months. And yup, you guessed it, the same situation occurred! He slowed down in payment and eventually stopped paying altogether. Again, another $5,000 lost. I didn't learn from my first lesson. Looking back on this second situation, I realized he had been having trouble getting funding. He was paying his employees more slowly, too. After we stopped working together, I found out he owed employees substantial back pay and, as a result, he lost his entire staff. He then started to bus employees in from a poor area of town to do telemarketing for him, and he ended up not paying them either — only this time the employees did not give up as easily. They threw rocks at his rented office building and broke windows. Needless to say, the landlord threw him out of the building as well. I don't know what happened to him after that.

The importance of contracts

Trust your gut when you're looking for clients…and yet. BIG FIRST LESSON: When you're first starting your business, you want clients. Any kind of clients, it doesn't matter who! You're like a little puppy that's starved for attention. Once you get just a little bit of love, you go crazy and wag your tail, you look up longingly, you give a slight whimper of thanks, and you go to work — like a dog! You do anything and everything to please the client. You're so pleased they chose you to work with.

The client may say, "Oh, we don't need a contract, I know you'll do what you say you'll do…"Of course you will, and you'll do much more, too. That attention-hungry puppy is on the loose!

In fact, you might just be so pleased with yourself for landing this client that when you present a contract to them for the services you're going to offer and the client says, "We don't need a contract," you respond with, "That's okay...I trust you'll pay me...you're really a good person, Mr. or Mrs. Client...and I know you would never think of not paying me...everything will be fine...I know you would never hurt me...you know I'm new at this and you'll do everything you can to make sure I'm safe."

STOP! Ohhhhhhh boy, you're in for the wakeup call of your life! DON'T DO BUSINESS WITHOUT A SIGNED CONTRACT — no matter whom the client is.

Or maybe, at the first sign of trouble the client will say, "Boy, I can't afford to pay you that much money..."They'll try to negotiate a lower rate. And guess what? No rate will ever be low enough for them. Hold your ground. You came up with your rate for a reason, and you deserve to be paid on the fair terms you've laid out in your contract. Don't let anyone talk you out of it. You're worth it...and more.

Once you get accustomed to using contracts, you'll find that they really do help you navigate those potentially bumpy areas in business relationships. They also portray a higher level of professionalism and allow you to show good faith in your client's business as well as your own.

Contracts are very simple to create. **I recommend finding a good general business** **attorney** who will be looking out for your best interest, and have him or her write a general agreement for you. This is a very inexpensive endeavor, probably no more than $200 and well worth every penny. Once you have your basic contract you can build from there. Most contract language is the same from company to company; the main differences would pertain to the specific services you're offering to the client and your payment terms. Remember that an attorney handles law and you handle the business side of the contract. If you can find a good attorney that will also provide some sound business advice regarding the contract, you have found a gem and a great asset for many years to come. Keep that attorney close at hand for all contract matters. You'll be much more confident in all your offerings knowing you're protected.

If you do find yourself in a position of being taken advantage of, it's important that you don't build a shell around yourself. Even if you run into a bad incident, don't shut out the rest of the world and distrust everyone and everything around you because of it. Many people do this in their personal as well as professional lives. This will stifle your business as well as your relationships. That shell will prevent you from fully trusting or giving of yourself entirely to your business or to others. Let your relationships and business flow naturally. You'll find both will grow much more quickly that way. Forcing a direction that isn't natural will stymie your growth.

WHEN YOU LOSE A CLIENT

I'm sorry to have to say this, but as a business owner, you're going to be rejected many, many times. It happens, so deal with it and get over it and keep moving forward with your life!

Not too long ago, I came home from a wonderful vacation. I was all nice and rested, ready to take on the world. Big plans were rushing through my head for the day ahead of me. I thought, "Well, let me get the emails out of the way tonight so I don't have to go through a bunch of them in the morning. That way I can get started with a fresh day based on my newly laid plans."

So at 10:00 p.m. that evening, I started doing just that. I got halfway down the list of emails in my inbox, when I noticed one from a vendor I work with. As I've previously mentioned, one of the divisions of my company sells health insurance. As I looked at the email more closely, I saw that it was a Broker of Record letter — basically known as the "kiss of death" in that industry. In essence, the vendor had very kindly notified me a few days ahead of time that my client would no longer be using my services.

I read the email and my head started to spin. I felt light headed. Panic set in. I simply could not believe my eyes. This client was a dear old friend of mine, too. I had helped him through some tough times, and he had helped me. We were close. We even sang in the church choir together! What really hurt was that he didn't even have the balls to call and talk to me and tell me he was looking at another broker. Did I not pay enough attention to him? What had I done wrong? What could have I done better? This was terrible!

I quickly called his cell phone (even though it was 10:00 at night). He didn't answer. I called him again the next morning at 7:00 a.m. — he didn't answer. The panic was still there — the hurt, the shame of losing a client. It was as if I had lost a friend. And hadn't I?

Analyze what happened

When you do lose a client, you'll need to analyze why you have lost them. If you can get them to talk to you, ask them questions that will allow you to improve your service the next time around. But don't lose your head over the situation, because no one benefits from this.

I have chosen optimism, even when I've lost a client. As long as I know that I have done everything in my power to properly service that client, and they still leave, I'm fine with that. I believe that the loss of a client provides me with another opportunity to build my business for the next client. I have had two clients leave. Each time, I interviewed my clients to see what I could have done differently. In both situations, the clients had been thrilled with my service, but the owner wanted to go back to the previous relationships for reasons outside of my control. Lesson learned — always maintain strong relationships with the head decision maker.

Then move on

But back to my original story. Throughout that night and into the next day, I continued to berate myself, until I finally said to myself, "WOW — OK!!! STOP!!! Holly, stop beating yourself up — and stop harassing the client! Guess what? Everything happens for a reason. It's time to move on to the next client. You can learn something from the loss of this one, but you cannot learn anything if you're wallowing in self-doubt (fear) and ranting and raving. And maybe you don't even need to learn anything! Maybe you didn't do anything wrong! Move on; don't sit in this pathetic puddle of self-pity. There is a bigger plan for you than where you are now. There is a *better* plan for you than where you are now. Don't waste any more time on this case. It's time to make your money elsewhere. Lift yourself up by the bootstraps, Holly, and move forward. That means now!!!"

So after I got over my little self-indulgent pity party, I started to turn my thoughts around to the positive and the future.

When you lose a client, take one minute and beat yourself up...and then move on. Don't wallow in self-doubt and self-pity. If your client found someone else that fits their needs better, let him go at it.

You'll lose some clients. And sometimes it really hurts, especially if you've put your heart and soul into the relationship. This is when optimism comes in handy — to see the bright side and to understand everything happens for a reason. This is also why you need to diversify and have many clients rather than one or two big ones. BIG LESSON TO LEARN: I cannot emphasize this enough — never, ever have just one big client. Your company is too special to let one client dictate whether or not you should be in business. If you cannot immediately start your business with more than the one big client, aim to expand your client base within six months of opening your doors. You don't want your company to be only as good as your next sale.

Always remember, today is a new day, with new services and new products to offer and new clients that will be a better match for these products and services!

Hire the Right Employees

(DINI) As quickly as possible, expand your staff. You can't do it all by yourself. **Make sure you hire the right number of people**; too few is just as bad as too many. For example, if one employee is responsible for a big portion of your success, realize that if that person leaves, your company could be in jeopardy. You might consider breaking the critical parts of that single position into two separate positions, to minimize the risks of relying solely on one person. But whatever you do, don't take on that extra responsibility yourself so that you're doing the work. You'll never expand your business that way.

When hiring any individual or outsourced company, trust your instincts…but also make sure you have an agreement of services in writing. We'll talk more about trust in the next chapter.

WHO TO HIRE?

Look for someone who complements you

Don't hire someone who is exactly like you. You need to hire people who provide different levels of expertise than you do. And yet when hiring anyone, regardless of their expertise, you'll find that it's still important to make sure that they fit within the culture of your company. If they don't, you won't be happy, they won't be happy and production will suffer.

Hire a product development expert

Your employees must be committed to growing the revenue of your company. The first step to revenue growth is making sure you have a high quality product…or hiring someone who has the expertise to improve your product. If your product isn't of high quality, you'll lose clients quickly and gain a poor reputation in the community and market place. Word spreads quickly!

Hire a rainmaker

Second, hire someone to help you sell. Especially if you don't like to sell, this person will be extremely critical to getting your company off the ground quickly. In fact, I highly recommend that you hire someone who can service *and* sell — with an emphasis on sales. Many times it's hard to find one person with both of these skills, but I'm telling you from experience, you don't want someone who services and refuses to sell. In my opinion, even when you start to build out your firm and you have more service people, you'll still want your service people to sell — this criterion is essential for the continued growth of your company. Your service people must also understand how to upsell products as much as possible.

I prefer to pay my sales people a base rate plus commission or a draw. Typically, if someone is commission only, I find that they don't stick around long. You must help them provide a living for their family, which usually means giving them a fair base salary so they don't have to worry about where the next dollar is coming from and they can then fully concentrate on your company.

Keep in mind that any employee you hire, especially in the beginning, must be able to bring in revenue to the company. Every employee needs to understand that the success of the company depends on earning more clients. Even the person in charge of product development is selling. Without that individual making your product better, you have nothing to sell.

Hire administrative help

The third person you should hire is an administrative person who can perform a multitude of tasks. He or she becomes your support. If the HR fairy also happens to bring you someone with a talent or even a liking for sales, that would be great as well! You might find someone just starting out or just getting back into the workforce who would like to be in sales but doesn't have the sales skills yet, and that's fine. You or your salesperson can teach them the skills that will help grow your company.

Ensure loyalty

Make sure your people are dedicated to your company. I cannot tell you what a great feeling it is when all of your employees believe in your company as much as you do. It feels wonderful to know you have built something that can help other families build their lifestyles, have homes, provide gifts to their loved ones or whatever money does for them, while also knowing that they have a real pride in where they work.

At our company, we don't consider work to be work. We consider it fun! We enjoy the continual growth of our company, the dream we all share, and also the flexibility. My employees know what needs to be done and they do it. I want my employees to be able to do what they need to in business as well as with their family, without feeling tied to a job or a desk. For me, it's important that each employee live a full life that expands beyond work. This philosophy builds trust between my employees and me. I trust they will put in as many hours as it takes to get the job done, and they know I don't question their work schedule because the job is getting done. Good working relationships like this are essential.

CONSIDER OUTSOURCING

Hiring full time employees can be expensive, but outsourcing someone as a 1099 subcontractor allows you the flexibility of having someone there only when you need them — especially when you're building out your products or services. You might only need a person in the beginning start-up phase of your company; therefore, outsourcing this position would be advantageous. Then when you no longer need their services, you can easily discontinue the services until you need them again.

Be careful with outsourcing and the legal requirements for 1099 status; make sure the person you subcontract with meets all of the criteria.

DO YOUR HOMEWORK

What is a "gut" instinct? It's your inner awareness that tells you if something is right or wrong. How many times have you not trusted your gut instinct and found an ending you wish you hadn't found? Trusting your instincts hits every aspect of your business, from hiring the right people, to choosing the right clients, to picking the right vendors to support your company.

Trust your gut. Don't hire someone you don't feel comfortable with.

Let me make one additional comment — get a background check on every person who might work for you. It won't be foolproof, but a local or state check can definitely help your confidence level in your hiring decisions.

Make sure all your employees or outsourced personnel sign a non-disclosure agreement and a non-compete agreement. You don't want them taking your clients or confidential product or company information to the next job. This is imperative. Again, no matter how much you trust an individual, it's not's personal, it's business. And a good business practice is to have every employee sign both of these agreements.

Find the Right Vendors

CONSIDER THEIR BUSINESS PHILOSOPHY

Look for vendors that share your business philosophy. At my company, we look for vendors who are honest, down-to-earth individuals who look out for us just as much as they look out for themselves. You should know that a vendor is looking out for your best interests, and that they want a long-term relationship with you.

Hiring fellow entrepreneurs as vendors is also a great way to help others as well as to promote small business in America. I find that fellow entrepreneurs are easier to do business with, and I enjoy the opportunity to build long-term business relationships with these like-minded people. If you can help the vendor build their business and they can help you build yours, I say why not! You'll also have the satisfaction of knowing you have helped someone else get to the next level in their business. This is called giving back, which is essential to success in business.

Having said that, it's also still important to take all the steps you can to protect yourself and your company in case something goes wrong.

PAY ATTENTION TO THE FINE PRINT

Never pay in full in advance

It's critical that you don't pay a vendor the full amount for their services until you have received the full benefit. Many vendors will ask for payment in full up front. Don't do this. At the most, pay for half the service up front with a promise to pay the rest at the end of the deliverable. If you don't, you'll never get your money back if you're dissatisfied.

Always have a signed contract

Vendors are a very important part of your business, no doubt about it. You must have confidence that they will provide the services they are proposing. It's fine to trust your instincts, but always make sure you have a rock solid contract in hand as well. You may go through a number of vendors trying to find the right fit for your company; that's completely normal.

Try to use your contract, not theirs

When entering into a signed agreement with your vendors, it's preferable to have them sign your agreement rather than you sign their agreement. At a minimum, make sure your attorney reviews the agreement they want you to sign. No matter how familiar you are with contract language, always run these agreements past your attorney. After all, that's what your attorney is there for — to protect you. Don't worry about the additional attorney cost; trust me, your attorney will save you money in the long run.

Make sure any vendor that you do business with signs a nondisclosure agreement as well. This protects you from them disclosing any of your company information or product or services details to anyone else. This protection is essential.

Negotiate Like a Pro

At some point in owning your business, you're going to have to negotiate for something. Whether it's over the salary you want to pay a new hire or for the best price from a vendor, negotiating skillfully will be important to the success of your business. But negotiating can be extremely nerve-wracking to many of us… and even to seasoned pros! Most of us simply don't know how to negotiate well because we never learned. Negotiating skills are not usually taught in school and probably not something you picked up at home or during your childhood, either. And there's often a healthy amount of fear holding us back, too. But remember, fear is typically caused by not knowing all the facts. You must clearly understand both your side and their side of the story before you can negotiate from a position of power. There are many ways to look at any situation, so let's discuss how to figure this out. As long as you know the whole story, I promise you, there are no surprises in negotiations.

Negotiators are generally happy people. Once you get used to negotiating well, you'll notice that you can ask for things you never thought you would ask for — and that you'll get them, too! Soon you'll find that you're obtaining things you never thought you could have…when all along, all you needed to do was to ask. The more you open yourself to opportunities, the more you'll find that negotiating can be your best friend.

But there are times when poor negotiating skills can prevent you from achieving what you desire. Have you ever been in an argument where you got defensive and immediately became weak in doing so? Did you back yourself into a corner with no ability to win? Did you become angry, or did you react in the opposite way and just give in? Did you become emotional and lose focus on the end result you wanted to achieve? If any of this sounds like you, then it's time to strategically build your negotiating skills into the effective machine you need.

Negotiation comes into play when two or more parties have a difference in opinion on the ultimate outcome of any given situation. Winning a negotiation means that all parties are in agreement and, in some way, everyone wins in the final outcome. Your role in assuring the negotiation is favorable to you is to **use** the following five negotiating tactics:

PREPARE: Know your position, their position, and every position in between

PORTRAY: A positive attitude and body language

LISTEN: Keep communications open

TAKE THE HIGH ROAD: Always be honest

PUT IT IN WRITING: Never leave the table without a written agreement

PREPARE

Prepare, prepare, prepare. Before you begin any negotiations, remember that the person who understands the issues the best will be the strongest. One of the reasons people fear negotiations is because they fear what they don't know. They fear that someone may know more than they do, or that someone may know something that didn't occur to them, or that the other party might say no to their requests. The more you understand about a situation, the easier negotiation becomes. Play both sides of the board. Understand not only your side, but theirs as well, and all the other choices that could occur in the middle. Understand that there may be more than two answers to any situation.

When developing a negotiation plan, make it simple. Remember, in every negotiation there is a beginning, middle and end. Understand each step and know where you want to be.

Be open

The more you believe there is only one solution for you, the more you'll be in a losing position. Why? Because your mind becomes so focused on one outcome, that you cannot accept any other position. Thorough research of all the options will provide openings you may have missed because your mind refused to see them. Ever hear the saying, "You can't see the forest through the trees?" This is what we are talking about here. If you're too focused on one particular outcome, you could be missing an even bigger or better outcome. Make sure you look at all your options.

Before you begin, know where you are and where you want to be. You'll get more of what you want in the negotiations, because you'll have developed a clear path in your mind toward the end result you want.

Set your initial offer

Carefully set the parameters of your initial offer before you begin your negotiations. Depending on the situation, set the parameters either higher or lower than what you would expect to obtain, but set them realistic enough so they still entice the other person. You set one end of the negotiation zone; the other party sets the other end.

Remember what is driving you; is it the price or is it a principal you're negotiating? If price is the driving factor, know where you want your end number to be. Set your negotiation zone and don't go beyond it against your favor unless another factor plays a stronger role.

Build support for your position

Knowing the reason for every aspect of your offer greatly enhances your chances of success. If you have a reason for your stance, then it's more likely that you'll get what you want. That's why it's critical to prepare and know your justification every step of the way.

If you don't have a reason to hold your particular position in the negotiation, then you begin to lose credibility and ground. This is also when you could become emotional, because you're floundering for a solid rationale for your next step in the negotiating process.

Go first or second

What's the best order? It depends on the situation. Going first may give you the power to set the parameters to your benefit. Or maybe you're in a situation where you want your opponent to go first; you never know, they may come in at a better place than what you would have thought. They may also provide additional information that will support your side of the negotiation. So look at the whole situation before you commit to going first or second.

Be realistic

When negotiating, you want to set expectations that are high enough to present a real challenge but realistic enough to promote good working relationships. It never hurts to ask for more than you think you'll get, especially if you can back up your position as to why more makes sense. You'll be amazed at the results.

Above all, never take things personally. This is business.

Plan to make concessions.

While preparing for your negotiations, identify in advance those areas where you would be willing to make concessions. Note that when you're willing to make concessions (not get run over), you'll find that it triggers the law of reciprocity.

When you give, the other person will tend to want to give as well, until soon you'll reach agreement with the other party. Have you noticed that when someone gives something to you, you have a tendency to want to give something back? More times than not, people want to reciprocate.

Also, know that you won't always win on all of your points. Part of preparing for negotiation is understanding which points are the big ones on which you cannot give in, and which points you're willing to give away. Know that doing your homework ahead of time will make it easier to win on most of your points.

Negotiating isn't a matter of convincing your opponent to concede, but it's instead an opportunity for you to provide information to help the other party understand why your position is the correct one. You may not win on all the points, but make sure the ones you do win are the ones significant to your goals.

Each side needs to see the satisfaction of movement in their direction. Choose which areas you're willing to concede before you negotiate, and have a strong story as to why the points you're going to keep remain.

Leverage

Negotiation leverage points include: needs, wants, competition, and time. These factors can be used as leverage either against your position or in your favor. For example: If you crash your car, and you **need** another car right away, you have less leverage because of the need and because of **time**. Therefore, you may not get the best deal. Also, let's say you **want** a particular type of car — and it's a particular unique color that is only available at one dealer. Last, there are two other people who want the same car — **competition**. In this particular scenario, your bargaining power would be greatly diminished! Always look for these four leveraging points; you'll be surprised to know that the other person will likely be experiencing at least one, or more, of these factors as well.

PORTRAY

It's important to be positive both in your attitude and in your body language throughout the negotiations. How you come across is 90% of negotiating successfully. Words are not nearly as important as actions.

Face-to-face negotiations can be much more effective than over the phone or in writing. The reason is because the body speaks for itself.

Posture

We all have our own natural way of standing or sitting. Some of us may have developed the habit of slumping or hanging our shoulders over the years.

When entering negotiations, posture is one of the first things someone will notice. You don't want to look tense, but you also don't want to look like you're not attentive to the situation. You want to look like you're in charge and ready to move forward.

This means shoulders back, head sitting square on your shoulders and looking straight ahead. Keep your arms to the side and your hands relaxed. Be careful not to cross your arms — even if it's a natural posture for you. In negotiations it closes you off from communications with the other person. Also be careful not to cross your legs. The more open your stance the more open the communication will be. You're in charge — keep your posture in charge as well.

Watch your opponent; where they may be closed at first, you may notice them opening up as you begin to formulate the negotiations for them.

Handshake

This is the beginning of any negotiation, so make sure your handshake is strong and firm. This one touch will immediately let the opponent know what kind of person you are. If your handshake is weak, half-hearted or condescending, your negotiations will already be off to a bad start. A strong firm handshake is what's needed.

Positioning

Depending on the negotiations, you may want to make yourself look larger. If so, try standing instead of sitting. Standing can also represent a higher status. Even if you stand now and again, you'll show that you're comfortable in your space and that you feel at ease in your negotiations.

If you're sitting, you can still portray an image of power. If standing isn't appropriate, try to take up more space by stretching your legs out or by having your arms at the side of the chair. This can also show openness. Keeping your arms to the sides of the chair shows that you're relaxed.

If you're on the phone during negotiations, a change in positions can be perceived. For example, when standing up to get a point across, your voice will reflect the change and support the message you're trying to convey.

Head movements

Do your best to keep your head steady. Sometimes we have a tendency to show agreement to statements when we don't mean to do so. Showing agreement before understanding the situation weakens your position. It may also cause you to inadvertently agree to something that isn't in your best interest! Instead of simply nodding without thinking during the negotiation, listen attentively, analyze the data and respond to it.

Nervous habits

Nail biting, playing with your hair, squirming in your seat, making off-handed comments or jokes, or adjusting your clothes — take all of these and any other nervous habits you have and put them away. Each one of these habits displayed during negotiations will weaken your position. Add to that list nervous hand movements and tapping of a pen as well!

Eye contact

Direct eye contact is best in negotiations, even if this isn't your normal way of conversing. Direct eye contact means power. Shifting eye contact means uncertainty or distrust. People can feel messages very quickly based upon how well you connect visually.

Matching and mirroring

The more you match and mirror the other person, the more they feel that you have their best interest in mind. This type of mirroring can range from something as overt as gestures to something as subtle as matching how a person is breathing. In fact, if you really want to get subtle, watch the other person's pupils; if what you're saying is affecting that person strongly, their pupils will dilate!

LISTEN

Listening keeps communications open

Without communication, there are no negotiations; things simply become a push and shove match. If you simply state your side without listening to the other side, your position is weakened. If you become argumentative, you lose. Laying down your cards without understanding the players and their positions weakens your position and your ability to negotiate. Once the communication bridge is burned, you'll pay Hell getting it back.

Any time you're communicating in business, whether it's during a negotiation or in the middle of a sales meeting, listen 80% of the time and speak only 20% of the time. You may think that negotiations require you to speak more. However, you'll find that the more the other party talks, the more you learn of their position and the easier it becomes to retain your position.

Silence is also a negotiating tactic. If you remain silent after your offer, especially if you let the silence linger for a few minutes until it begins to feel uncomfortable, you can sometimes get what you want. Just be aware that the other negotiator may try the same thing with you!

Find out more

The more you work with the other negotiator, the stronger your negotiating stance becomes. Always be honest and respectful in your negotiations. This will be remembered during and after negotiations. Since you have already done your homework, there should be few surprises. Listen carefully and always make sure you understand their position by asking questions and obtaining clarification before you respond.

You'll want to develop questions prior to your meeting. The questions you ask must be thought-provoking and must help you to understand the other party's point of view. Once you have developed this list, obtain as many answers to the questions prior to the negotiations as you can. These answers will provide to you the ammunition you'll need in your negotiations. Remember this diagram from our discussion of high gain questions? Use the same principles to outline your questions and answers for your negotiations as well.

TAKE THE HIGH ROAD

If the other negotiator becomes argumentative, the best approach is to let them talk themselves out and simply take notes. This will keep you from getting emotionally involved and will give you time to gather your thoughts. Listen carefully and verify that you understand their position. Sometimes just this simple verification brings the negotiations closer to your position, just because you *listened*. Sometimes that's all people want to know — that you've listened to their side of the story. It's a powerful feeling to know that you've really been heard.

On the other hand, the argumentative negotiator may be using this as a tactic to get you to bend. Don't. Let them talk themselves out and actively respond through verification of your notes. This reiteration of their side disarms them.

Remember, you're looking for a long-term relationship here; that means finding ground where both parties can come out winners. You might even give the other party a small gift prior to the negotiations, especially if you sense hard feelings of any kind. This helps to break the ice and smooth the process.

Negotiations include a series of turns until finally both parties come to an agreement. Most importantly, trust must not be broken within negotiations. Things may feel strained if they're not handled properly. That is why doing your homework and understanding both sides of the negotiations will eliminate most, if not all, of the issues.

Give to get

Be trustworthy and honest in your negotiations. Be fair. If others are unfair to you, let them know. Don't allow unfair treatment. This will break down the relationship, so confront the issue immediately. Generosity begets generosity. Fairness begets fairness. Unfairness brings about a lack of trust and a break down in the relationship.

When negotiating, if you give something away once, don't give away anything else until the other negotiator gives you something in return. Sometimes we get nervous and think we need to keep talking, when in actuality you already gave and already talked plenty.

Always take turns. After you make a move, wait until the other party reciprocates before you move again.

CLOSURE

Put it in writing

Once you have both come to an agreement, put it in writing, right then and there. Make sure there are no misunderstandings. If the close is emotional for either side, take this into consideration as well. Remember there is no room for emotions in negotiations, so if you're the one who is emotional — gain control or finish the negotiations when you can control your emotions. DON'T close the deal if you're not in control.

Make sure all concessions are in writing and that you and the other negotiator sign off on the agreed-upon terms. This isn't a time to rush, but instead to make sure both parties are in agreement. You both should be satisfied with the end result. Finalize the agreement and move forward without delay.

EXERCISE 4.4

Think of either a past situation or one that may be coming up for you that will require negotiations.

- What do you want?

- Where do you begin your negotiation?

- When do you make a move?

- How will you close?

Now think about your opponent.

- What do they want?

- Where will they begin their negotiation?

- When will they make a move?

- How will they most likely close?

CHAPTER 5

CONGRATULATIONS — YOU'RE AN ENTREPRENEUR

Take the Lead

I would like to start this chapter with a story from a client of mine, Kevin Murphy, an entrepreneur who a year ago started Solutions Mechanical in Burr Ridge, Illinois. In this first year of business, the company has grossed $1 million dollars. I asked him to share with you how he accomplished that, and here is his story:

"I started out as a field technician and was fortunate in that I was able to learn from some of the best in the field. I quickly rose up through the ranks and became the top technician at the company I worked for. At the age of 27, I left that company and joined one of the top firms in Chicago, where I was able to build up a $1 million division.

I credit my success to my parents who told me to always work hard and put your heart into everything you do. When I was a kid, my parents used to every now and then take weekends away, just the two of them. They would always bring us kids back a souvenir. One year when I was eight years old, they brought back a plaque for me that had a picture of a sled dog team and read, 'If you ain't the lead dog, the scenery never changes.' I held onto that plaque, but it wasn't until five or six years later before I started to get it. I finally understood what it meant — that if you're not a leader, then all you're doing is following someone else's dreams. From that point on, this saying became the driving force in my mind. The plaque became gold to me.

I wanted to take risks and chances on my own — and that I did, one risk after another. After building one company for someone else, I left there and worked for one of the largest industrial manufacturing plants in the area — a $100 million company. I worked for and reported directly to the owner, but we constantly butted heads and so I left. I left also because the company had changed. They didn't seem to care anymore about the clients or the employees. Everything and everyone became a number to them, and that's just not how I do business. My moral compass was being compromised, and I needed to get out.

I lead with my heart and the passion I feel in what I do. I believe that one of the most important things in business is to treat customers fairly. This whole service industry is built on trust and relationships. A standing rule in my business is to never lie to or misguide customers. We don't just put bandages on problems; we tell a client what's wrong and we fix it right the first time.

When I look at my priorities in life, God comes first, my wife and children and family come second and my business comes third. This is the way my life will always be aligned.

When I decided to start my own company, I contacted a good friend of mine who was also in the same industry, and together we created a business plan. Soon after, at a family party, my friend's brother introduced us to another friend who had just completed the sale of one company and was ready to venture into another. We showed him our business plan, which, frankly, impressed him; he agreed to invest capital into our new company — and he also became the head of marketing and sales for our company. This was a perfect fit; my friend and I covered the technical operations of the business, and he brought in the customers.

One of the keys to our quick success was that we were aggressive as hell when we went after potential business. In our first year of operations, we are at 150 percent of our projected plan. We started the company out of my home, which we soon outgrew; we now occupy a 400-square foot office. Our growth has been steady, and we've been cautious about how many people we've hired and who we've hired, as well as how many trucks and additional equipment we've purchased as we've grown. We offer extremely competitive rates for our services — we save our clients 20 to 30 percent – while at the same time we provide a level of service our clients have never seen before.

We utilize our own internal marketing call center, which provides enough leads to land one to two new customers a day. Our goal is to increase this to two to three new customers a day, and so on, as we continue to grow. We also send out direct mailings and obtain clients through the internet and repeat customers and referrals. In fact, our largest income source is repeat and referral business. Actually, I don't even ask for referrals; they just come. I know if I were more aggressive with referrals, this would increase my business as well. We're proud of our referrals; they only come when you prove your capabilities through action. A lead from a referral is one of the biggest compliments we can get. This is when we know we have done a good job.

My partner who manages the field, Randall, has been in the business a long time. He's a big guy with a huge truck. When he pulls up to a client's place, the client immediately gets a warm fuzzy feeling and feels confident that he will get the job done and fix their problems right the first time.

I know working with partners can sometimes be tough. We have monthly meetings and we don't always see eye-to-eye, but we get the job done. You just have to roll with the punches. And sometimes you might get hit with a left hook because we have three different people with three different opinions, and we're not always going to agree on everything. But as long as you keep the lines of communication open and have an honest debate, then you'll find that you can all work together.

As we built our business and talked to different people about our needs, we found ways to get our offices furnished for hardly anything. A conference table and dry erase board were given to us, as well as enough furniture to fill the space for only a small amount of money rather than thousands of dollars. If you look for people to help you, you'll find them. Also, look toward family. We used my family as well as my friends' families to obtain free services to build our website as well as the technical infrastructure of the company. I also thank of one of my clients who gave us a break. He had started his own company a number of years back. He hadn't graduated from high school; he did odd jobs and eventually started his own company in the car business. He now owns a multi-million dollar company. This man is one of the kindest, most down-to-earth people I know. He gave us all his business, which was our first real chance to begin our company.

I guess what I'm saying here is that you have to have the brass balls to go out and make it happen. If you think you can — you will. I found it interesting that the people I had worked for prior to all of this actually knew before I did that I was going to start my own company. You'll be surprised to find out that you've been building your vision all along, even if you didn't know it yet.

It took us only one week to start our company. We stayed up many nights and built out what it would take to service our first clients — from creating work tickets, to calling old contacts that we could connect with right away and close. We sent out to those early clients a promotion that they couldn't resist…and we were in business. In fact, the promotion went so well that we have extended it to all our clients as an additional incentive for their loyalty.

This year, we held our first Christmas party at the office. As we were toasting our success, my partner Randall looked at me and simply said, 'This is cool.' I knew exactly what he meant. Here we were — our own company, and now we were responsible for building another family here, of employees and their families who were dependent on our success and were just as committed as we were to the success of the company.

Many people tried to talk us out of starting our own company, since we were doing so during the worst economy I have ever seen in my life time. People would ask me why I would leave a perfectly good job where I was making lots of money and had secure benefits. Why take the chance? But I would take that negative and turn it into a positive (the true entrepreneur's mindset!) and I would tell them that I don't want to be the big corporate junkie who only cares about the bottom line. Or as the plaque states, 'If you ain't the lead dog, the scenery never changes.' "

 EXERCISE 5.1

For the next week, note the decisions you make trusting your "gut" instincts. Note how natural those decisions feel and how you react more quickly. Do not second guess your choices — simply make the choices and move forward.

Practice doing this every day. So many times we over-analyze our decisions and then lose the momentum necessary to move forward. Make a decision and stick to it. Move forward. Consciously make a mental and (if possible) written note each time you trust your instincts in making decisions, whether in your personal or professional life. Note how often your instincts are the correct first decision and how often they are not. You will be surprised how often you are right.

Understand the Importance of Systems

The other day I talked to a friend whose area of expertise is operations; he has partnered with his brother to take over and turn around an old family-owned business. Now, it turns out that this business hadn't made a significant change in 15 years. They'd survived all these years thanks to the "good 'ol boy network," but the network was starting to dwindle and new faces were coming in. Their accountant was so archaic he was still using a DOS operating system and faxed over profit and loss statements to the two brothers that they could hardly read. The company had no policies or procedures in place at all. In short, the company was a mess.

The brothers brought me in to help with a problem employee, and as a result of that work I developed an employee handbook. But I could see that the problems were big and that these guys needed help. Luckily, the ownership wouldn't completely transition for another year, so the new owners had some time to shake things up.

Now, you would think that since my friend and his brother were buying the company from their immediate family, there would be some mutual sharing and caring, but apparently not in this case. The brothers had only a vague idea of the financial situation of the company, and they found numerous mistakes in the commissions. The company tracked sales in only a very limited way, and they literally did not know which salespeople were bringing in the business and which were not. They were not able to track revenue or even look at sales patterns. Also, the current owners hadn't ever automated the payroll system because occasionally they needed to float payroll for a couple of days to stretch their cash flow. It seemed like they had been spending more time hiding things than actually doing business!

There's a lesson here: Whether you're looking to start your own company or looking to buy, make sure you closely assess the systems that are in place or that you'll need to put in place to protect your interests and track your sales. Needless to say, automation is a must and a problem that needs to be quickly resolved. In this story, this company didn't have any type of accounting system, except for a few random Excel spreadsheets. Clearly, it was time for a change.

If you're intending to buy a company and it does have systems in place, make sure you understand the costs of the systems. Some people pay way too much for accounting software, for example, and these costs can actually outweigh the benefits. Be mindful and realize that systems are tools to save time, improve accuracy and increase sales. If the cost of a system is more than the revenue it brings in, get rid of it.

My friend and his brother are going about this change in ownership in the right way. They are looking carefully at the profit and loss statements, they are automating systems, and they are beginning to protect their interests by instituting policies, procedures and non-compete agreements. All they need now is guidance — which I'm providing to get them to the next level, and soon they will be well on their way to a profitable business.

Surround Yourself with Expertise

I was speaking to a fellow entrepreneur not too long ago about the anxiety that can pop up when you own a business, and I asked him what has made him anxious as a business owner. He admitted that he had been preoccupied lately trying to get his business' financial house in order.

I share the same anxiety. Let me tell you right now that I hate working on the books. Love making the money — hate reconciling everything. This is the same feeling this fellow entrepreneur had, but he didn't want to spend the money on outsourcing this part of his company. However, he also refused to work on the financial stuff during crucial business hours because he realized if he spent the time working on the books instead of making additional income or building his business, he would be wasting valuable time. (This is known as desperately trying to work *in* your business and not on your business!). So instead, he would work on the books at night or very early in the morning. He was sacrificing his own free time — which only shows that time is never really FREE.

He used to enjoy working out in the morning, but he had to stop because he needed that time to work on the books. He used to go to networking events or spend time with his family in the evenings, but now he wasn't doing that either. Pretty soon he was losing self-confidence, losing his energy, losing his focus. It seemed the harder he pushed, the further behind he got. Eventually his family and his employees became fed up with him. This formerly high-energy entrepreneur ready to conquer the world was instead being conquered by an internal battle.

Finally, after four grueling weeks of going through the books, he had almost finished the task — when he made a single errant keystroke on the computer and accidentally integrated his file with another one, and the data was irretrievably damaged. Now he was back to square one! After several hours of major self-pity, he realized he had just learned a very valuable lesson.

1. You cannot work 16 hours a day and expect to love what you do.

2. You must exercise, eat right and get enough rest or you won't function at peak performance.

3. If you don't stop and smell the roses now and again, people will not want to work for you.

4. Outsource those areas of your business that you're not good at or the areas that keep you working in the business — doing tasks — instead of working on the business — being the lighthouse for future growth.

I believe there are three key business functions you need to outsource. And I've asked my favorite experts to help me explain why.

YOU NEED AN ATTORNEY

Brent E. Ohlmann is my attorney. He's based in Naperville, IL, and I have found him to be excellent counsel and a great resource both when I was starting my business and since. I asked him what entrepreneurs should know about attorneys, and here is what he had to say:

"Why hire a lawyer? To have the benefit of the attorney's experience with similar business clients, and to understand how to use the opportunities the law provides to both avoid common problems and to take specific, smarter approaches. Having a lawyer isn't a luxury that should be put off until the business is successful. Getting good, focused legal advice is a critical part of starting up any new business and is often worth much more than what you pay in terms of peace of mind and understanding alternatives on how to run the business. Identifying, understanding and addressing legal issues aren't things you can do by buying a 'form' from a website.

How should a new business owner select a lawyer? I think most professionals are found through word of mouth or referrals from others whom they trust, like a commercial banker, accountant or business owner. Hiring a lawyer is like choosing a doctor. You need to be comfortable with speaking candidly and trust that the lawyer is giving you honest advice, not just telling you what you want to hear. Many lawyers have clusters of clients in certain fields or industries, and you may want to find someone like that who is familiar with the nature of your business.

Although we don't use the U.K. labels of 'solicitor' and 'barrister' to categorize lawyers, most focus their practices in either handling transactions and preventing problems, or going to court and litigating problems that cannot be resolved amicably. Forming businesses, preparing contracts, and giving advice about what laws govern your business and how to use them to your advantage is what transactional lawyers do.

I tell most new businesses that if at all possible, own your business by yourself and hire or contract with talented people to help you run it. I have seen many partnerships that began with best friends — until an unresolved conflict between the partners killed the business outright, crippled it by scaring off employees and customers, or, worse yet, drained both partners' resources with a court battle."

YOU NEED A CPA

Make sure you have a CPA or accountant in your back pocket, and make sure they are reputable. Your CPA will become almost a part of your company, so look for someone who will give you more than just tax advice; you want someone who can act as a business partner. You want them to help you understand how to run your business and to be willing to give you free advice now and again.

(As a side note, always ask your preferred vendors — such as your attorney and CPA — for referrals. My CPA is also my client!)

Christina Klein is my CPA. She is a partner at Klein, Hall & Associates, LLC, a licensed CPA firm in the Chicago area. One of her company's specialties is helping small businesses with their taxes. I asked Christina what advice she would give to companies just starting up. Read carefully what she says to look for in an accountant. Do this right the first time and you'll save lots of headaches in the future!

"The first piece of advice I would give is to hire people to do what you don't want to do. Especially hire an accountant and don't try to do payroll by yourself. This is an area many employers have difficulty with and end up losing money by not having an expert doing it for them in the first place. If you make a mistake on taxes or if you pay taxes late, you could end up in a lot of trouble. The cost to hire an accountant or payroll service to do this for you is minimal in comparison to the cost of the penalties.

At Klein, Hall & Associates, we have put together a packet for start-up companies that answer a lot of common questions. Check with your accountant for the same.

Also, pay your own bills, at least for the first year. Even if you outsource this to someone else eventually, make sure that you review every bill so you know where your money is going and how much everything costs to run your business.

Make sure you understand how to read a profit and loss (P&L) statement. Know what a P&L is and how to use it in your business. It's important to track expenses and know where the income is coming from and how to build upon it.

Never co-mingle personal and business accounts. A good example of this is when you first start your company you won't be able to get a credit card, so you'll have to use a card with your personal name. Even though it has your personal name, if you decide to use it for business then don't use it for anything but business. A business is required to have separate accounting books and records. Not doing so causes an accounting nightmare and pierces the liability protection your corporation provides to you personally. If you're sued and your personal and corporate funds are co-mingled, then they could sue you on a personal level as if you were a sole proprietor because you're not treating your company separately. Think of it this way: If you worked for a large company, would you mix your personal expenses with your employers' expenses? Of course not — so keep them separate, even if you're small.

Hire a bookkeeper. They can keep things straight on a month-to-month basis for you. The cost to have them do this may be $100 a month, which is a lot less than having a CPA straighten it out at the end.

When looking for an accountant, look for a licensed CPA. A licensed CPA is licensed by the state and must meet certain educational levels. Hiring someone who states they are a CPA isn't the same as hiring someone who is a 'licensed' CPA — make sure they have that extra distinction. Ask them if they are part of a peer review program; this is where a peer visits the CPA's office and checks to see if the CPA firm is doing their work correctly. This peer review only occurs for licensed CPA firms, and it provides protection for you as well as a way to effectively monitor practicing licensed CPAs.

Many times at Klein, Hall we will obtain clients who have been with a non-licensed CPA, and the books are a complete disaster. It's important to keep your books in order. Keep in mind, if you're looking for a loan, the bank will ask you for your financial statements. By using a licensed CPA, you'll have everything in order.

Also understand that just because you hire someone to do your taxes doesn't mean you're not responsible for them. This is also why you want to make sure you have hired someone who does things right the first time. Many people don't have the credentials and that could cause a problem for you.

As of 2011, the government has improved protection for people who out-source their tax preparation. In order for the preparer to be able to sign your tax return, they must be a licensed CPA or must take a test to show that they are legitimate in their knowledge.

Make sure to call around for prices, and make sure that the accoun-tant isn't going to bill you every time you call and ask a question. An accountant should never bill you for asking questions or for correcting the mistakes that they have made. I recently received a new client because another firm was doing just that. In fact, the client had wanted to switch accounting firms for a couple of years, but because the firm had all of his information, he thought it would be difficult to switch. Not at all. People think it's hard to switch accountants, but it's not. All you need is last year's tax return, and the new accounting firm is on its way."

YOU NEED A TECHNOLOGY EXPERT

Russ Schuller, owner of Simple Solutions Technology in Chicago, explains tech-nology and your business in simple terms below:

"Often times when an entrepreneur starts a new venture, they become overwhelmed by the technology needed to run the business. But aren't computers and technology supposed to make your lives simpler and more efficient? These things shouldn't get in the way of running your business.

The two most common mistakes I have seen new start-ups make from a technology perspective are under-preparing (what I call the "Ostrich" approach) or over-preparing (the "Buzz Lightyear" approach). The goal is to prepare smartly and to fit your plan to your needs (the "Fits Like a Glove" approach).

The Ostrich ignores technology because it's intimidating. Instead, the Ostrich may choose to record transactions in a paper logbook, advertise only in the Yellow Pages or the local paper, maintain a single set of records kept on-site, etc. This can leave the Ostrich missing out on a world of opportunities, in terms of being accessible to potential clients. This outdated approach also means the Ostrich spends much more time each week performing manual tasks than other businesses. And finally, this approach leaves the Ostrich vulnerable to the risk of not having a reliable backup plan for critical company information in the event of a disaster.

Buzz Lightyear, on the other hand, over-prepares with all the latest and greatest gadgets. He tends to purchase far more technology than he really needs. I have seen companies in various disciplines that insist on buying only top-of-the-line versions of computers, firewalls, networking equipment and internet service packages, when they really only needed half of that to effectively run their business and still allow modest room for growth. This approach leads Buzz Lightyear to an infrastructure that is expensive to setup, difficult to maintain, and often goes under-utilized.

The Glove comes in with the mindset of identifying precisely what is needed to effectively get the business going while being careful not to needlessly overspend. For example, if you want to tighten a screw, you need a screwdriver. You don't need the whole hardware store. The Glove knows that easy-to-use applications sufficient for handling necessary business tasks are a must. Also, the Glove adopts smart technology best practices, like a simple and secure network design, systems to track and forecast sales, and local or off-site backup of critical information.

There is no need to be intimidated by the technology you need to run your business. It is possible to find the right fit for your new venture without overspending. Just take the time to, first, identify the core business functions that can be automated or computerized, and second, either research the best solutions for those needs or ask your technology expert for help. Having a good relationship with a qualified technology company is important.

So in the end, wisely choosing your technology and leveraging it smartly can make all the difference in your new venture, not only by making you more efficient so that you can focus on your core business, but also by opening up many opportunities for networking and gaining access to the thousands and millions of your potential customers. Strategic use of technology will allow you to learn what you have done well and what you can do better in your business, so that each year is better than the last.

Congratulations on being one step closer to your successful new venture!"

But sometimes, even if you've surrounded yourself with all the right expertise, you still need to make business decisions by following your own instincts. What roles do trust and ethics play for the entrepreneur? What should you know ahead of time? Read on to find the answers!

TRUST AND ETHICS

At every single level of your company, trust is the number one pin that holds it all together. If you find that you're working with someone who isn't trustworthy, it's imperative that you immediately terminate the relationship and learn from the incident. Assess what you may have missed as you were building that relationship. Identify the characteristics you noticed about the person with whom you were working, and try to look out for those characteristics in the future to keep this from happening again. Make no mistake, it will happen again, but always study the situation and see what you could do differently to avoid it in the future.

Jim Carr, a dear friend of mine who owns Blue Book Services, Inc. in Carol Stream, Illinois, teaches business ethics and management at Wheaton College in his spare time (where he gets the time, I don't know). Jim recently shared some thoughts with me on the importance of reading people and trusting your instincts.

"Blue Book Services, Inc. is the credit and marketing authority for the fresh fruit and vegetable industry, as well as the lumber industry, throughout North America. Anyone who desires to do business in either the lumber or the produce industry checks the Blue Book for up-to-date rating and marketing data.

What is particularly fascinating about the produce industry is the way they trade — mostly over the phone, where business is conducted on the value of your word, all the way from the growers to the end users.

You can learn a lot from this approach when you're considering hiring someone, too. Look for substance, and try to see what is deep inside a person. Trust your gut and ask penetrating questions to find out more about the person and what his or her expectations are in terms of working with you.

Realize too that their resume is only the tip of the iceberg. Try to take into account how and where he or she grew up. For example, a friend of mine came from an abusive childhood. Nevertheless, he grew up, went to college and became involved in education, first as a teacher and later as a principal. He was a man of outstanding integrity, and he treated people the way he wished he could have been treated. He looked out for the welfare of children and tried to make certain that their lives were filled with love, compassion, and quality education. It would have been easy for him to have gone in a different direction, but because of who he was as a person, he decided to turn a wrong into a right.

Look for an individual who has passion and dedication to what you do and to the ideals set forth via the culture of your company. An individual who works for you who has no passion or dedication will likely not make it, at least not for very long, in your work environment. Jim Collins, in his book *Good to Great*, calls this 'getting everyone on the bus.'

'Ethics' refers to one's moral compass or, better defined, it's the 'North Star' that never deviates. When you look up into the sky, all you need to do is find the North Star, and you know which direction is north. Don't veer from what you know to be true. We each have a North Star inside of us.

In the produce industry, clients need to maintain a certain rating if they want to advertise in Blue Book publications. If a firm's rating happens to fall below the rating threshold, the firm is no longer able to advertise. We can draw a parallel from this to all business as well. In other words, just as there are standards to be met for a firm to advertise in Blue Book publications, so should standards be met in all businesses. Integrity and trust are two of the standards which are hallmarks of doing business in the produce industry, and they should be the standards for doing business in all other industries as well.

One way of looking at ethics, from 30,000 feet, is to take into account the 'gray' area of life, which is where economics, law, and religion intersect. For some issues, there is no right answer. For example, look at how some businesses treat labor as a commodity. A commodity of course refers to a thing, such as a chair, typewriter, car, computer, etc. Should the labor of a person be considered as a 'thing' or a commodity? Professional athletes are drafted right out of college and traded from team to team, much like cattle that can be bought, traded, or sold. Certainly there need to be rules governing this process, and indeed there are. And yet, a great deal of money stands to be made from the drafting and trading of professional athletes, while the law puts limits on the behavior. These are the 'gray' areas of life where easy answers may be elusive.

Over the last few years, many people have received pink slips, as layoffs and firings have driven the unemployment rate very high. Businesses have had to take these steps to get their financial houses in order, or in some cases, just to survive. However, when someone is losing a job, how you convey the message is important. A text or an email advising a person that he or she no longer has a job is very cold-hearted. Managers should at least take the time to meet with each person individually, face to face. It's the right thing to do.

Trust and integrity should be the cornerstones of doing business. From another perspective, trust and integrity are essential to acquire information so that better business decisions can be made.

There is no question that ethics have been stretched and pulled as the economy has brought very large corporations, such as General Motors, to their knees. Nevertheless, in good and bad times, trust and integrity will always help to make certain one's moral compass never veers from true north."

Thank you, Jim, for your insightfulness on trust and ethics. Your life-long endeavor to always find justice has paid off.

Risks and Optimism

I was at a conference a few days back, and I was speaking to someone about this book and how I was giving a jump start to fellow entrepreneurs. Her comment to me was, "Ohhhh, do I have stories to tell about that!" She explained how she had tried getting into her own business but fell short because she was constantly trying to perfect her business plan. Every time she started to implement the plan she had on paper, something would not go according to this plan she had so carefully mapped out — so she finally gave up. She didn't realize that even the best laid plans will always change, and in fact, this change is what makes the plan real and makes an actual business come to life. She hadn't prepared herself to handle that risk.

There are always risks in anything that you do. For that matter, from the moment you step out the door and hop in your car, you're at risk. I can say though, if you have an aversion to risk and if you're not confident, and change becomes an overbearing issue, then you're probably not ready to run your own company.

Risk can really get the blood flowing and bring you to higher levels of thinking and management of your business. If you know you want it, then push past the risks and move forward.

BUSINESS PLANS

I do agree a business plan is important (there is a sample for you on my website, **www.uconnectsite.com**). But I don't believe that if you don't have one you should stop yourself from going into business, nor do I believe you should expect that things will go as planned. Even before you have your business plan, begin the steps you've laid out toward building relationships and working to get your first clients. Many people get so hung up on planning that they fail to ever take action. An old-school millionaire I spoke with once said memorably, "If you have to go to business school to learn how to do business, then you have no place in going into business!" I thought that was very interesting. And he's right. School doesn't make a business man or woman. At the same time, school sure does open your eyes and exposes you to a lot of things you might never learn how to handle otherwise. In this day and age, I would always recommend getting your bachelors and masters degrees in business, if you can. They are tools that will help you in your business, and they give you immediate credibility.

That said, don't let the lack of a degree hold you back for one minute. Don't let anything hold you back!

OWNERSHIP LEGALITIES

I'm not a big fan of going into business with a partner. Too many times I have seen partners split and then you have nothing…or half of nothing. Of course if you go it alone you may have to take out loans to get the financing you need, and you'll have to deal with the ebbs and flows of cash management by yourself, but always, always keep control of your business. Ownership of my business is one of the top four things I hold dear in my life. First come my daughter, my husband and my family, but then comes ownership of my business.

Owning my own company gives me a feeling of security I cannot feel working for any other company. If I'm working for someone else, I'm never sure when someone will come along and eliminate my job. To me, I gain security by knowing that I make my job and my life any way I want, and I can build or destroy it any way

I want without the help of anyone else! All you need are those first few customers that will bring in the initial income to get the ball rolling. Once it does, you're on your way to success.

DON'T IGNORE YOUR BUSINESS

If you're looking to be a consultant, be careful not to let your clients eat away all of your time. Consulting means you're spending time on someone else's business — not your own. It means building their business — not your own. Unless you can easily duplicate yourself, it's tough to be a full-time consultant. Find something that allows you to grow *your* business while growing the client's business, too. I know, because I've been there. Projects can take hours, days, months, years — and yes, you're getting paid during that time, but to have a successful business you must always be thinking about where your next dollar is coming from. Planning for future growth has to be your top priority — which is difficult to do when all of your time is spent working for your client.

DIVERSIFICATION

DON'T put all your eggs in one basket. Build a strong base, client by client, but be careful that one client doesn't take up too much of your time. Your time is limited, especially if you're a one-man or one-woman shop, so don't spend all of your time on one client. I don't care how big the company is. If they drop you for someone else (which more than likely will happen sometime during your lifetime!) then you'll have nothing left.

I can't tell you how many small companies I've talked to that went out of business during the latest recession, especially marketing companies. If you look at corporate America, when there is a downturn in the economy, who are the first people to be laid off? Typically marketing people. This may be a good opportunity for outsourcing, but it's also an area where people stop spending any money for a period of time. I know — it's crazy, since the whole point of marketing is to get your message out to the public so you can sell more!

A corollary to these recent layoffs is that a lot of entrepreneurs leave the parent company and start up their own business, but their only client is the company they just left. Except now, they're subcontractors, and the company doesn't have to pay expensive benefits. Trust me, that is NOT a good deal for you! The company let you go or you left them. Now they hire you whenever they want to, and in fact, they have you so wrapped up, you can't go out and find more clients. Not good! If at all possible, keep the big clients happy, work on their stuff on off hours — but keep your prime time open for prospecting and building your business.

Moral of the story: Get out from under that "false wing of protection."

Just as it's important to have more than one client, **I also recommend having** **more than one product or service line.** Yes, I know many experts out there will tell you to focus in one area and stick to it, but look closely at your future. Will your product be around ten years from now? Will it be replaced? A prime example in my own experience is what's been happening in the health insurance industry over the last five years and what is still to come. Eventually, brokers will not be necessary. More and more, sales will be made online, and health care reform will continue to move forward as well. Learn from this example and diversify your business now, before you're facing challenges to the product you're selling. Minimize your risk and look for other areas into which you can expand.

PRODUCT IMPROVEMENT

Today one of my salespeople asked, "How can I sell something if it's broken? If it's not working perfectly? If everything isn't just right, how can I sell it?" I said to her, "I have been selling products for more than 20 years, if not for myself, then for other companies large and small, and I can't tell you that I ever sold anything that didn't have a few bugs in it." Okay, that might sound like a sloppy comment or an easy out, but it's not. When you're inventing something or building a product, even if you have spent thousands of hours or many years on the product, there is always going to be a fly somewhere in the bottom of the wine glass. I prefer to look at that fly as an opportunity. An opportunity to take that glass and throw it out, and pour a bigger and better glass for myself and have enough to give to others as well!

Don't get frustrated with the issues and the setbacks in building a product. Those setbacks usually mean you need to take a step back and fix the problem. The solution is a bigger and better solution than the one you had before.

Case in point: My company built a software program that integrated a company's contact base with a VOIP phone, so that calls and emails could be automated and the history of each client or prospect phone call or email could be easily stored. The system worked fine when a company ran a single marketing campaign, but our clients wanted and needed to run multiple campaigns with multiple scripts simultaneously — and they were having problems doing so with our software. I had just hired a new programmer (since my first programmer ran off and took the code to the program with him — dummy me — nothing like having one employee in charge of and holding onto a code that cost you $300,000 to build — hopefully you'll learn from my lesson!) to fix the problem. After he spent a month fiddling around and rebuilding the code, he realized that the code had never been built to handle more than one campaign at a time. Because we discovered this problem, we were able to rebuild a bigger and better solution. Wow — how important was that?

I know this may sound obvious now, but at the time, when we were rifling through coding and technology that is to me a foreign language, it was difficult to see ahead to the end result — a deliverable that more clients could use. The lesson I learned was to never be afraid of complaints. They can only make you stronger.

Actually, I learned many lessons from building that product. I learned how important it is to take an initial risk so that you can get to the next level of risks and do a better, smarter job the next time. I learned the importance of spreading out responsibilities across several people instead of paying one key person a high salary. I learned that you should trust your gut and to always take your dream as far as it will go. Even though this product did not make the money I had hoped for, I felt good that I had pushed it to the limit and that I had taken that product as far as I could. I learned strength. I learned that a belief in yourself will build your passion even stronger. I also learned to never give up, even if the product or service you're offering takes a dive. Go back to the drawing board and start again.

This is also why diversification is so important, so that you have more options down the road if you need them. Testing the market with different products will lead to success in one or multiple markets.

You have a business to run, and that means you need control over where your business is coming from to ensure a continual flow of revenue. This may mean you need to change your approach! Remember, you are what you do. If that means excellence, great. If it means anything other than excellence, it just means you have room to improve.

CHAPTER 6

FINAL WORDS

Take Out the Trash

Your thoughts are not you.

All day long, we entertain random thoughts. Our minds are filled with things we should do, things we didn't do, things we could do, our past, our present, our future...until our minds are so full of trash we can't think straight about the things that are actually important to us.

When we finally decide to sit down and do what is important to us, we find more trash in the way preventing us from accomplishing anything of value. Why?

Because we're afraid we aren't good enough.

Because we're afraid of what other people will think.

Because we're afraid someone else could do it better.

Because we're afraid it's too big of a project and we'll never get it finished.

BECAUSE, BECAUSE, BECAUSE!

This world is so big, and many times (as mentioned before) we just don't see the forest through the trees. We don't see the big picture, the bigger picture or the biggest picture beyond that. We get so caught up in our own lives we lose track of everything around us.

Stop the noise in your head. I tell myself, "TAKE OUT THE TRASH!" And guess what? It starts to clear out. But I have to remind myself all the time. It doesn't come naturally for me. The more you remember to say this to yourself, the clearer your mind will become. You'll be amazed by how much more you can do and how well you can do it. Stop trying to do it all — especially all at once. You know the drill for success: Pick an action, write it on your calendar, stick to the plan and don't get distracted. Get rid of all the small stuff that keeps you from your goals. TAKE OUT THE TRASH! Do it this moment — here and now!

The tough part is that it takes wisdom to throw out what you don't need. **So train yourself to become conscious of your thoughts, actions and reactions.** Keep your mind empty of anything you don't need. Eliminate all the "woulda, coulda, shoulda's." These are only empty thoughts that hold you back from your dreams. Don't let them enter your head, and when they do, simply tell yourself, "TAKE OUT THE TRASH."

Your mind has a tendency to develop habitual ways of handling things, particularly stress. Some people shut down, some throw in more obstacles to build a wall of defense, some get angry, while some simply see the stress and push right through the middle of it. I used to react in all these ways until I learned that pushing through the middle of the stress is most effective.

Stay in business; don't go back. You chose to be a pioneer, so don't give up the dream which is now reality. Venture out and make this life your own, not someone else's dream. Stop asking someone else to live your life for you. YOU are in charge — not corporate America or anyone else. You own the business, you make the decisions, and you take the glory!

Live in Optimism

The most important thing to remember is that this is just a moment in time — and that, yes, this too shall pass! No matter what happens, always stay the eternal optimist — because everything happens for a reason.

If something bad has occurred, analyze what happened and then move on, because whatever it was can help you get to the next level in your business. If you've lost a client, it's because you needed to focus on a different type of client or you needed to improve your customer service or your clients wanted you to introduce a different product line — who knows, but take it as a sign that good things are coming around the corner.

If something good has occurred, take a moment to celebrate. But then still analyze what happened, and move on to make the results even better next time. Always keep improving and keep looking forward to what's coming around the bend!

Actually, see if you can figure out the next move before it comes! Over time and with practice, you'll start to see the patterns in your life and you'll be able to predict your next move. Understand and enjoy every move you make as you reach for your goal. Life is too short to not enjoy every moment of it. Don't spend your time in the stress zone, when there is so much happiness to experience. Plow through the middle. Look ahead, work in the moment, and always stay positive.

When it comes to the influence of others, it's good to listen to suggestions, but make sure that your end decision is based upon your dream and your passion. I guarantee that if you're doing what you're doing because of someone else, then you won't succeed to your fullest capability. Something else will get in your path to pull you away from what you're doing. And that something else will probably be what you should be doing.

Sometimes we get a start in business and we then find that the product we want to offer doesn't generate enough money to make a living. As we discussed in the previous chapter, consider adding another product or two to shore up your business until your passion can be realized. Just don't let the new products pull you so far off the path that you never get around to your actual passion.

On the other hand, if you start your business with a product that you know will make money but is not your passion, first find your passion within that product and then continue to build on it. You'll eventually have a strong enough foundation to continue building out your passion in another area as well.

I started my company by selling health insurance and by building a lead generation software program to help increase sales closures. This company has been very profitable, and it has allowed me to do what I've always wanted to do — help people like you become entrepreneurs. For me, this was my own destiny telling me I needed to make money first before I could feel secure enough to live my passion. Should have I done it the other way around, and started with my passion first? Maybe. But that's the beauty of the world. You choose your own path.

Just Do It!

Don't waste your time trying to figure out the world — just do it. Move forward. Listen to others, but don't let them control your life or your business. This is your business and it will flourish under your control.

We entrepreneurs work long hours, but we don't even notice because we are doing what we love. This is our passion, this is our company. The excitement and synergies come together, and it's an amazing experience.

I am living the dream. Once I realized that, I also realized that all of a sudden the resources I needed would always come to me.

Stop for a moment and close your eyes. Hear everything that is going on around you. Realize that the world is continually moving, and you always have choices. The tasks that you have set before you are just that — tasks that YOU *have* set before you. You don't have to be on this journey. If it's too tough, then move in a different direction. If it's not your passion or your dream, then move to a brighter path that isn't so clouded with obstacles.

(DINI) **Every day I ask for guidance for the day to come.** As I mentioned earlier, I have developed my own form of Jabez's Prayer that I use in different areas of my life. I'll sometimes change the words slightly depending on the situation, but its meaning is always the same — to go beyond my wildest dreams! My version goes like this:

> "Oh bless me, Lord, bless me indeed and enlarge my territory. Place your hand upon me. Keep me from evil. Keep me from causing pain."

This little prayer covers a lot of things for me. It starts by asking for a blessing, which can be in any form that you want. If you don't believe in a God, then ask for a blessing from the Universe — it's a big place, you know! The purpose is to get your mind off of yourself and into the world around you, praying to something larger than yourself. Many times we are so caught up in our own little worlds that we forget about all the beauty that surrounds us.

Next, "enlarge my territory." When I say this, sometimes I stretch my arms as wide as they can go to emphasize both size and thought. What I envision is a great big oak tree I sit under now and again, that I've named Rosemary after a close relative of mine who died after many years of suffering with rheumatoid arthritis. This woman went through more pain and more operations than I could ever imagine, but she always had a smile and a kind word. So, like the sheltering arms of the big oak tree, expand your branches — your mind — wide, to let in as many people, thoughts, and opportunities as you can in that day. Stay focused on your mission rather than everything in between.

Third, I ask that the Lord place his hand upon me to protect me. This is like a security blanket. It takes away some of the fears about going out there on your own; you have someone or something watching over you.

"Keep me from evil" is pretty self-explanatory. I always think of the clients that said they would pay but I ended up $5,000 poorer. Lord, keep me away from the crooks!

And finally, "Keep me from causing pain." Help me to help my employees and clients make sure I'm honest, forthright and living by my company mission of Service above Self.

After saying this prayer, you'll find that many more things will come your way. If you don't like this idea, create your own special words — anything that takes you out of yourself for just a minute or two so you can reconnect with the big picture and see beyond your everyday issues.

You're on this path for a reason — now is the time for you to take action. You have all the tools you need to begin your business, so don't delay. This is your moment. This is your day!

INDEX

INDEX

INDEX

INDEX

INDEX

INDEX

INDEX

INDEX

INDEX